entire question
WD

Vocabulary
in practice 5

40 units of
self-study
vocabulary
exercises

Liz Driscoll
with Glennis Pye

with tests

CAMBRIDGE
UNIVERSITY PRESS

CAMBRIDGE UNIVERSITY PRESS

Cambridge, New York, Melbourne, Madrid, Cape Town, Singapore, São Paulo

CAMBRIDGE UNIVERSITY PRESS

The Edinburgh Building, Cambridge CB2 2RU, UK

www.cambridge.org
Information on this title: www.cambridge.org/9780521601252

First published 2005
Reprinted 2005

Printed in Italy by Legoprint S.p.A

A catalogue record for this book is available from the British Library

ISBN-13 978-0-521-60125-2 paperback
ISBN-10 0-521-60125-8 paperback

Contents

To the student

This book will give you the chance to practise your vocabulary in a fun way.

Vocabulary in Practice 5 has:

- 40 units of short, enjoyable exercises – each unit practises groups of words which belong together
- 4 Tests – one after every 10 units, helping you to remember the words from those units
- an Answer Key
- a Word List – this is a list of all the words in each unit with information about how the words are used.

You can use the book in two ways:

1 Start at the beginning of the book. Do units 1–40 and then do the Tests.

2 Look at the Contents. Do the units you think are important first. When you have finished the book, do the Tests.

You can do each unit in two ways:

1 Do the unit and check your answers in the Answer Key. Study the Word List and learn the words you got wrong. Then do the exercise again.

2 Study the Word List for the unit. Then do the unit and check your answers.

Note Do the exercises in this book in pencil. Then you can do the exercises again after a week or a month. Repeating the exercises will help you to remember the words.

Here are some ideas to help you to learn vocabulary:

- Write new words in a notebook: write the meaning in English or in your own language, then write a sentence using the word.
- List other related words: noun, verb, adjective [e.g. assertiveness/assert/ assertive].
- Write the words in phrases, not in isolation: adjectives with nouns [e.g. immediate family], verbs with nouns [e.g. make a promise], words with prepositions [e.g. related to].
- Note anything particular about grammar [e.g. irregular verb form] or usage [e.g. slim (positive), skinny (negative)].
- List words in groups: words with opposite meanings [e.g. extrovert/introvert, make money / lose money], words with similar meanings [e.g. relation/relative, run-down/shabby].

We hope you find this book useful and that it makes learning English words fun.

1 Names

A **Read what the woman is saying and then complete the form with the words in the box.**

> Hi! I'm Jean Jarvis. Actually, my full name is Jean Frances Jarvis but I don't like the name Frances, so not many people know that. I didn't much like my name before I got married either – I was Jean Smith then and that was a bit boring.

first name	maiden name	middle name	initial	signature	surname	title

APPLICATION FORM

1 .... (Mr/Mrs/Ms/Miss) *Mrs*

2 .... *Jean*   3 .... *F*

4 .... *Jarvis*

5 .... *Smith*

6 .... *Jean Jarvis*

B **Complete the sentences with the words in the box.**

anonymous	autograph	false name	married name	nickname	pseudonym

1 It is believed the attacker is dangerous and that he may be using a

....

2 An .... letter in connection with the murder was received. Police are working to find out who could have sent it.

3 Although she and her husband have been together for many years, the famous author has never used her .... The author explained: 'I was already known as a writer before I met James and it seemed silly to change my name to something no-one would know.'

4 In school my .... was 'Legs' because I was so tall.

5 In the nineteenth century it was thought that women should not be writers, so Mary Ann Evans was forced to use a male ....

6 The fans pushed and shoved, all hoping to get the player's

....

2 Family

A Match the underlined words with the definitions below.

There are six of us in my immediate family — I have three siblings, and my parents are both alive. My sister is adopted, so she's not actually related to me. But as far as I'm concerned, she's just the same as my two brothers. My dad was an only child, so he hasn't many relatives. But I still have a large extended family on my mum's side, because she was one of eight. Out of all my friends, I'm definitely the one with the most relations.

Every year we have a big family gathering. All the generations are there — from my great-grandmother who's very old now right down to some of her great-great-grandchildren, my cousin's children. I should know all my close relations, of course, but I don't always remember what they're called. Forgetting names runs in the family — we all do it! Distant relatives — like my grandmother's cousin's son — have no chance!

1 stages in a family history   *generations*

2 a family meeting or party

3 brother(s) and sister(s)

4 members of a family

5 parents, children, brothers and sisters

6 not near in a family relationship

7 including family members such as aunts, uncles, cousins

8 someone without brothers or sisters

9 near in a family relationship

10 of the same family

11 taken into a family and treated as their own by law

12 is found very often in the family

B Are these sentences true or false?

1 Your father is one of your siblings.

2 Your brother and your cousin are the same generation.

3 Your friends are usually related to you.

4 Your immediate family is usually smaller than your extended family.

5 Your grandmother is a distant relation.

6 Your distant relatives always live a long way away.

3 Describing character (1)

A Complete the lists.

adjective	noun		adjective	noun
1 assertive		7		capability
2 committed		8		competitiveness
3 conscientious		9		decisiveness
4 enthusiastic		10		motivation
5 organised		11		reliability
6 ruthless		12		self-assurance

B Complete the advert and letter of reference with the adjectives which match these definitions.

1 loyal and willing to work hard
2 wanting to win very much
3 not afraid to say what you want or think
4 very confident about your abilities
5 not caring if others suffer
6 able to plan carefully
7 can be trusted
8 puts a lot of effort into work
9 interested in and energetic about work
10 able to make decisions quickly and confidently
11 able to do things effectively
12 wants to do her work well

❓ Are you any or all of the following ...? ❓

completely (1) _____

highly (2) _____

absolutely (3) _____

100% (4) _____

really (5) _____

If the answer is yes, call this number now for more information about a job which could be just what you've been waiting for.

Kelly has been working as a secretary with Kopac Services for the past three years. She has shown herself to be a highly (6) _____ person who is (7) _____ and (8) _____ at all times. She has always been an extremely (9) _____ member of the team. Her ability to be (10) _____ at all times has meant that she has thrived in what can often be a stressful work environment. Kelly is a most (11) _____ secretary. As she is also highly (12) _____ , she has the potential to succeed in her future career.

4 Describing character (2)

A Complete the sentences with the words in the box.

aggressive	bossy	considerate	emotional	extroverted	gullible	
indecisive	introverted	materialistic	moody	open	placid	
secretive	stubborn	trustworthy				

WHAT'S YOUR STYLE?

We can tell a lot about someone by studying their handwriting. For example, it is said that untidy handwriting can tell us that person is (1) _____ , finding it difficult to make decisions. Handwriting which slopes to the right can be a sign of an (2) _____ person who is frequently angry and even violent towards others. And handwriting with no dots over the letter 'i' may be that of someone who is (3) _____ , a quiet person who may have problems making friends.

We asked an expert to look at several handwriting samples and here's what she had to say about them.

What can you tell about a person from their handwriting?
This person is an (4) _____ person who cries easily. It's someone who hides their feelings and plans from others – someone I'd describe as (5) _____ . It's also someone who believes almost anything they're told – a very (6) _____ type.

What can you tell about a person from their handwriting?
Looking at this balanced handwriting style tells us that this person is very (7) _____ , always happy to talk about their feelings and thoughts. It is the writing of a (8) _____ person who makes an excellent friend, always loyal and honest. They have a gentle, (9) _____ nature and are (10) _____ , often thinking of how others might feel or what others might need.

What can you tell about a person from their handwriting?
On the other hand, this is the writing of a (11) _____ type who refuses to change their opinion. It's that of an extremely confident and (12) _____ person. This is someone who enjoys telling others what to do – I'd call them (13) _____ . This person would be difficult to live with, a very (14) _____ type who often gets annoyed for no good reason. They also think that money and possessions are more important than anything else – (15) _____ is the word I would use to describe that aspect of this person's character.

5 Describing appearance

A Put the words in the box into two groups.

| lanky obese petite plump skinny slim stocky well–built |

big/fat   **small/thin**

....

....

....

....

B Match the words from A with the descriptions.

1 She's tall, with a large, strong body.   ....

2 He's too fat, in a way that is unhealthy.   ....

3 She's very thin in an unattractive way.   ....

4 He's short, but strong and heavy.   ....

5 She's short, with a small body.   ....

6 He's thin in an attractive way.   ....

7 She's tall, but very thin.   ....

8 He's a little fat, but in a pleasant way.   ....

C Complete the sentences with *build* or *figure*.

1 My elder cousin has the .... of a rugby player.

2 The actress had a beautiful slim ....

3 My mum has kept her .... quite well considering she's in her fifties.

4 Police are looking for a young man of slim but muscular ....

5 My sister does a lot of sport and has a very athletic ....

6 I'll lose my .... if I eat too much chocolate.

7 We use .... to refer to the shape and size of someone's body, usually in connection with strength and muscle.

8 We use .... to describe shape, especially whether it is attractive or not, and usually only for women.

6 How you feel

A Circle the correct words to complete the sentences.

1 The driver became <u>grateful / suspicious</u> when the customs officer started asking questions about what was in the back of the truck.

2 I was <u>furious / offended</u> with him. He had promised not to say anything and then went and told everyone.

3 Nothing seems to have gone right recently, so I feel very <u>amazed / negative</u> about just about everything.

4 We were <u>delighted / enthusiastic</u> with their decision – it was exactly what we had been hoping for.

5 I'm much more <u>positive / impressed</u> about my future now that I've passed all my exams.

6 She was in love and felt <u>ashamed / reckless</u> – not caring what anyone thought or what happened to her next.

B Match the other words from A with the correct prepositions.

1 .... about   4 .... for

2 .... at   5 .... of

3 .... by   6 .... with

C Complete the paragraphs with the words and prepositions from B.

★★HOROSCOPES ★★★

Virgo 23 Aug-22 Sep This week, you'll be (1) ....
the successes you'll have. They'll be all the more surprising considering the difficult times you've been having recently – there's no doubt you'll be
(2) .... your change in fortune.

Libra 23 Sep-23 Oct You may not be (3) ....
the behaviour of some of your colleagues this week (one of them in particular will disappoint you), but if you manage to remain
(4) .... your work, making a particularly big effort, you'll receive the rewards you deserve.

Scorpio 24 Oct-21 Nov Think long and hard before doing anything unusual this week. You may find that a friend of yours will be
(5) .... your actions and will refuse to speak to you for some time. You risk feeling (6) .... yourself and wishing you'd never done it.

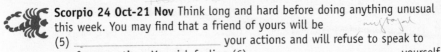

7 Describing things (1)

A Find twelve adjectives in the grid. Put them into two groups.

j	o	u	t	r	a	g	e	o	u	s	l	r	o	u	s	k	c
o	f	c	h	t	h	r	e	a	t	e	n	i	n	g	t	a	r
p	r	o	m	i	s	i	n	g	r	e	a	g	h	o	r	m	i
x	o	y	o	n	w	p	t	r	e	m	e	n	d	o	u	s	m
u	f	i	n	a	p	p	r	o	p	r	i	a	t	e	n	r	i
p	a	t	h	e	t	i	c	a	p	p	a	l	l	i	n	g	n
r	q	u	e	z	u	n	a	c	c	e	p	t	a	b	l	e	a
a	r	k	l	e	t	g	s	e	n	s	a	t	i	o	n	a	l
b	e	r	i	d	i	c	u	l	o	u	s	h	o	p	l	m	r

positive

....

....

....

negative

....

....

....

B Complete the sentences with the words from A.

1 If the result of a football match is .... , it causes a feeling of great excitement and interest.

2 If a dress is .... for a particular occasion, it is unsuitable.

3 If the price of a car is .... , it makes you very angry.

4 If someone's enthusiasm is .... , it is very large or great.

5 If someone's behaviour is .... , it is possible that something unpleasant will happen.

6 If a piece of work is .... , it is too bad to be approved of.

7 If a film or story is .... , it holds your attention.

8 If a restaurant looks .... from the outside, it looks as if a visit is going to be successful and enjoyable.

9 If the food in a restaurant is .... , it is very bad.

10 If a team's performance is .... , it is very bad, weak or useless.

11 If a suggestion is .... , it is very silly or foolish.

12 If the price of a house is .... , it is morally wrong.

8 Describing things (2)

A Circle the correct words to complete the adverts.

1
WOMEN'S hair drier, unused, still in its <u>high-quality / original</u> leather case. £10 only.
Tel: 01865 248978

2
SOFA in <u>eye-catching / handy</u> orange and brown, seats three.
£25.
Tel: 01325 35891

3
MEN'S ski jacket, large size, dark blue, detachable sleeves for warm weather, very <u>irresistible / versatile</u>.
Tel: 01865 311104

4
Keyboard with instruction books, CD and earphones, <u>ideal / stylish</u> for beginner.
Tel: 01865 246702

5
Video recorder VHS, black slim-line model, good working order, fair condition, great <u>practical / value for money</u> at £20.
Tel: 07866 8238868

6
PERSONAL CD-PLAYER, with <u>reliable / sophisticated</u> playback options, boxed and unused. £220 for both.
Tel: 01325 31793

B Complete the adverts with the other words from A.

1
GARDEN swing, suitable for children from 2 years, ... bargain at £15.
Tel: 01865 751613

2
FILIGREE bracelet and matching earrings, ... jewellery, but unwanted gift. £12 ono.
Tel: 01865 368013

3
TWO wall lamps, unused, brass/mahogany, very .... £20 the pair.
Tel: 01865 798181

4
COOKER, 50 cm wide, ten years old, very .... Too small for new kitchen. Accept £20.
Tel 01388 762569

5
WOMEN'S winter coat with hood, size 14 .... rather than fashionable. Worn twice. £25 ono.
Tel: 01325 700479

6
FOLD-UP bike, ... size for car boot or for carrying on trains.
Tel: 01748 822139

9 City life

A Match the underlined words with the definitions below.

This city, like any other, is <u>densely populated</u> and it can be difficult to decide which part of the <u>built-up area</u> you want to live in.

If it's <u>urban</u> living you're looking for, try the old <u>commercial district</u> in the centre of the city. Just ten years ago, this could only have been described as a <u>deprived area</u>. Many of the buildings were <u>derelict</u> or <u>run-down</u> until quite recently when a programme of <u>regeneration</u> began. Nowadays it's an <u>up-and-coming neighbourhood</u>, with several riverside <u>developments</u>, and property prices have risen over the past few months.

If you're in search of a <u>suburban</u> lifestyle, head for one of the <u>residential areas</u> several miles from the city centre. Some of the <u>suburbs</u> to the south of the city have modern <u>estates</u> with excellent <u>local amenities</u> as well as being within easy reach of the city centre.

1   no longer used and in bad condition   *derelict*
2   areas where people live outside the city centre
3   place where there are a lot of buildings
4   relating to cities or towns
5   not having the necessary things for a
    pleasant life
6   with a lot of people living close together
7   no longer in good condition
8   areas of new buildings
9   area of a city likely to be successful soon
10 part of a city with lots of shops and businesses
11 areas of housing
12 groups of houses built in a planned way
13 improvement of a place
14 nearby facilities that make life more
    comfortable
15 not in the centre of a town or city

B Are these sentences true or false?

1   Post boxes and phone boxes are examples of local amenities.
2   Many people work in derelict factories.
3   In most cities people don't live in the commercial district.
4   You find farms and parkland in built-up areas.

10 Housing problems

A Circle the correct words to complete the first part of the text.

More and more young adults are living together as sharers in houses and flats. This may mean that there is less of a (1) housing shortage / mortgage than originally predicted. While the news is positive, (2) deposit / homelessness still remains a problem, with a large number of families in bed and breakfast and temporary (3) accommodation / first-time buyer. More affordable (4) council housing / rent is needed for such families, plus (5) hostels / tenants for those forced to (6) evict / squat in empty buildings or to (7) home owner / sleep rough on the streets of the city.

B Use the other words from A to complete the second part of the text.

Jonathan Abram is 25 and moved here from New Zealand five years ago. He's lived in six shared households since then. 'My favourite home belonged to someone who was a (1) _____ and needed a bit of help to pay his (2) _____ which he'd agreed with the bank. There were six people living in the house altogether – five (3) _____ and the fellow it belonged to. The five of us paid (4) _____ for our rooms each month as well as a small (5) _____ before we moved in. I had an instant group of friends and it worked well – until the (6) _____ wanted the place for himself and his girlfriend, and had to (7) _____ us.'

C Complete the sentences with words from A and B.

1 A _____ has never owned a home before.

2 People who live in _____ often have to share a room.

3 A _____ is someone who has bought a house or flat.

4 There isn't much cheap _____ in many cities.

5 A _____ is someone who pays for the use of a room or rooms.

6 The money an owner borrows from a bank is called a _____ .

Test 1 (Units 1 –10)

A Complete the conversation. Write one word in each space.

A: First of all, what's your (1) _____ ?

B: Barrell.

A: Is that your (2) _____ name?

B: No, I'm single.

A: And your (3) _____ name?

B: Jania, that's J–A–N–I–A.

A: That's an unusual name. And what's your middle name (4) _____ ?

B: F – for Frances.

A: And your (5) _____ ? Ms?

B: No, it's Dr actually.

A: Thank you, Dr Barrell. Are you (6) _____ to Dr Nick Barrell?

B: Yes, he's a (7) _____ relative. I don't know him very well.

A: So, medicine (8) _____ in the family, does it?

B: Yes, lots of us are doctors.

A: Are there any doctors in your (9) _____ family?

B: Both my parents are doctors. But there are only the three of us. I'm an (10) _____ child.

B Circle the word for each person.

1 skinny / slim

2 obese / stocky

3 lanky / petite

4 plump / well-built

1   2   3   4

C Replace the underlined words with six adjectives from the box.

> appalling eye-catching handy original outrageous promising reliable versatile

1 The thought was <u>very silly or foolish</u>. _____

2 Her coat is <u>very attractive and noticeable</u>. _____

3 Her work is <u>showing signs that it will be successful</u>. _____

4 Your work is <u>too bad to be approved of</u>. _____

5 This bag is <u>able to be used for many different purposes</u>. _____

6 A mobile phone is <u>useful or convenient</u> on the train. _____

Test 1 (Units 1–10)

D The <u>underlined</u> words are in the wrong sentences. Write the correct word for each sentence.

1 My boss is <u>emotional</u> – he doesn't care about any pain he causes to other people.

2 She's being <u>aggressive</u> about her exam results – we don't know if she passed or failed.

3 If you disagree with him, he'll just argue back. He can be very <u>secretive</u> – and it's very unpleasant.

4 He's very <u>materialistic</u> about his work – he always finishes everything off before he goes home.

5 The bride got very <u>ruthless</u> at the wedding. She cried when she left for her honeymoon.

6 All she talks about is money – she's become so <u>conscientious</u> these days.

E Circle the adjective which describes how each person feels.

1 'I can't believe you took the money without asking!'   delighted / furious

2 'Wow, that's amazing! Did you really do it yourself?'   impressed / reckless

3 'I'm not saying it'll be easy, but I'm sure we can manage it.'   offended / positive

4 'Thank you very much for helping me with my car. It was very kind of you.'   amazed / grateful

5 'That'll never work. It's much too complicated and we don't have enough help.'   ashamed / negative

6 'This is great – I really love it. Everyone should try it!'   enthusiastic / suspicious

F Complete the paragraph. Write one word in each space.

I moved here five years ago. At first I lived in rented (1) .... in the centre of the city. I was one of four (2) .... in all, and we lived above a shop, in what wasn't really a (3) .... area – we didn't have many neighbours. The local (4) .... were great – there were shops all around us, and there were some great pubs too. But the man who owned the place wanted it for his daughter, so he decided to (5) .... us. I then moved in with my cousin and his family, who lived in the (6) .... But living four miles from my job in the city centre wasn't great – I had to get up much earlier. So in the end, my girlfriend and I decided to buy a place. We had enough money for a (7) .... and now we pay a massive (8) .... every month.

17

11 Modern living

A Complete the text with the words in the box.

commute   downshift   hectic   lifestyle   nine-to-five   quality of life
rat race   stress   under pressure   working conditions   work–life balance

Until recently, I didn't have a very healthy (1) ....
I worked as a publisher for a large company based in London, and I was
always (2) .... to meet deadlines and get the books
published. The schedules were really (3) .... last
year, and there was a lot of (4) .... in my working
life. Don't get me wrong, my (5) .... were fine. I
had a large office, with a beautiful view over the Thames. I had the latest
computer and a secretary too. In addition, I earned a very good salary. The
problem was that my (6) .... was completely
wrong. I was away from my lovely home in the country far too much. And not
only did I work very long hours, but I had to (7) ....
into London every day by train to get to the office.

   One Friday evening, after the journey home had taken me four hours
because of a rail accident, I decided I had to get out of the
(8) .... If I wanted to improve my
(9) .... and have more time for myself, my family
and friends, then I needed a (10) .... job which
would give me more free time. Next day I saw an advert for a sales assistant in
a local bookshop and put my house on the market. If I was going to
(11) .... , then I needed to make some economies
– and a smaller home was the first step. I've been working in the bookshop
and living in my cottage ever since!

B Circle the person who is more likely to do these things.

1 have a nine-to-five job – a taxi driver or an office worker
2 have more stress – a yoga teacher or a secondary school teacher
3 commute – an accountant or a gardener
4 be under pressure – a nurse or a ski instructor
5 find himself in the rat race – an office cleaner or a marketing manager
6 have a hectic day – a doctor or a museum attendant

12 Describing clothes

A Circle the materials and underline the patterns.

<u>spotted</u> (linen) wool <u>striped</u> silk <u>patterned</u>
<u>checked</u> cotton <u>plain</u> <u>flowery</u> denim lycra

B Match the materials from A with the lists of clothes they are often used for. Use each word once only.

1 .... cardigan, gloves, jumper, scarf
2 .... cropped top, cycling shorts, leggings, swimsuit
3 .... blouse, shirt, T-shirt, underwear
4 .... shirt, scarf, tie, underwear
5 .... blouse, hat, suit, dress
6 .... dress, jeans, jacket, skirt

C Match the adjectives from A with the patterns.

1 ....
2 ....
3 ....
4 ....
5 ....
6 ....

1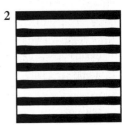

2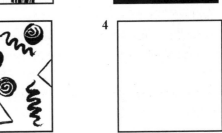

3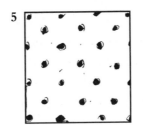

4

5 6

13 Fashion

A Match the underlined words with the definitions below.

I've been invited to a conference and a formal dinner afterwards and I'm wondering what to wear. I'll need something quite <u>smart</u> for the conference itself and an <u>outfit</u> for the evening, perhaps a trouser suit and blouse. But what should I buy? I once had a silk dress <u>made-to-measure</u> in Hong Kong, but usually I wear <u>high-street fashions</u> and buy them <u>off-the-peg</u>. I usually wear <u>casual</u> clothes, and would always choose a <u>garment</u> which was <u>machine washable</u> rather than <u>dry-clean only</u>. My sister-in-law, however, loves <u>haute couture</u> and has her favourite <u>designer label</u>. She always knows about the latest <u>trend</u> and has even been to Paris to see someone's spring <u>collection</u>. Perhaps I should ask her advice. On the other hand, she's got more money than I have, so perhaps I shouldn't!

1 one piece of clothing
2 clothes made by a famous designer
3 a set of clothes that are worn together
4 not suitable for special occasions
5 can be washed in a washing machine
6 clean, tidy and stylish
7 made specially for you
8 expensive clothes of original design and high quality
9 not made specially for you
10 clothes sold in shops
11 new development in clothing
12 can't be washed in a washing machine
13 a clothes designer's latest styles, shown every season

B Are these sentences true or false?

1 A suit, shirt and tie is an example of a garment.
2 People often wear casual clothes when they're relaxing.
3 High-street fashions cost more than haute couture.
4 You can wash dry-clean only clothes at home.
5 Made-to-measure clothes should fit better than off-the-peg.
6 A T-shirt and shorts is an example of a smart outfit.

14 Catalogue shopping

A Match the sentence halves to make parts of an advertisement. Write the letters in the box below.

PEDAL YOUR WAY TO FITNESS AND HEALTH FOR ONLY £199!

1 We *guarantee* next-day *delivery*

2 Otherwise, *order* processed within 48 hours

3 We will *exchange* any unwanted items by *return* of post

4 *Offer* subject to *availability*

5 Send your *order form* and *payment* details

a and not for despatch outside the UK.

b to *Customer Services*, JYK Bikes, Oxford OX27 3RW.

c and goods despatched within 14 days.

d for any *purchase* over £250.

e and *refund* the difference for any goods found cheaper elsewhere.

1 .... 2 .... 3 .... 4 .... 5 ....

B Complete part of an advertisement with the words in *italics* from A. Note that some words can be both nouns and verbs.

OFFICE FURNITURE
UNBEATABLE VALUE!

Allow 7–10 days for (1) .... from receipt of

order. If you are not satisfied with your (2) ....,

we (3) .... a money-back

(4) .... Simply (5) .... the

goods, undamaged and in the original packaging, within 28 days for a full

(6) .... or an (7) .... for another item.

(8) .... by phone or website, or complete the attached

(9) .... with your address and method of

(10) .... and return to our (11) .... department.

Alternatively, visit our new department store at **13 River Street, Cambridge**.

Please phone on **01235 678543** to check

(12) .... before commencing your journey.

15 Eating and health

A Complete the text with the words in the box.

> additives   balanced diet   convenience foods   eating habits
> fresh produce   GM foods   healthy eating   junk food
> nutrients   nutrition   organic foods   processed foods

One of the keys to enjoying a fit and active life is a (1) ....
A poor diet, on the other hand, is associated with an increased risk of illness. Two
thirds of natural deaths in the West are believed to be linked to diet, according to
leading experts in (2) .... and health. Medical authorities
have drawn up guidelines for (3) .... based on a large body
of research into diet-linked diseases throughout the world.

- Eat a wide variety of foods to get the whole range of (4) ....
- Limit (5) .... because most contain large amounts of
  sodium and other (6) .... Cut down as much as possible
  on (7) .... , such as burgers and chips, and
  (8) .... , such as ready-made meals from the supermarket.
  Eat or cook your own (9) .... – fruit, vegetables, fish, meat
  – instead. Where possible, buy (10) .... – produced without
  the use of artificial chemicals. (11) .... may not harm us,
  but they are not good for the environment.
- Change your (12) .... gradually.

B The underlined words are in the wrong descriptions. Write the correct word for each description.

1 <u>Vitamins</u> add taste and smell to food. Vegetable oils are
   unsaturated and the least harmful oil for cooking.   ....

2 <u>Water</u> is the body's most common source of energy.
   Found in bread, pasta, potatoes and rice.   ....

3 <u>Fibre</u> is needed to replace skin and hair, and to renew
   damaged cells. Found in meat, fish, milk, cheese, eggs.   ....

4 <u>Carbohydrate</u> is vital for flushing out waste products
   from the body.   ....

5 <u>Protein</u> fills you up and accelerates waste removal from
   the body. Occurs in dried fruit, nuts, beans.   ....

6 <u>Minerals</u> are organic chemicals which protect the body
   against disease.   ....

7 <u>Fats</u> are non-organic substances, vital to good health.
   Calcium and zinc are two of the most important ones.   ....

16 Money and banking

A Circle the correct words to complete the paragraph.

I've had my (1) bank statement / bank account with a bank in the local high street for ten years. This is very convenient and my (2) account number / deposit is very similar to my date of birth, so it's easy to remember. However, I've not always had a good relationship with the bank manager. I receive a (3) bank statement / deposit once a month, and this arrived yesterday. To my horror, my (4) balance / bank statement at the end of last month was only £3.47. I'd made a big (5) account number / withdrawal the previous week to buy a new bike. Fortunately, I get my pay cheque tomorrow, so I'll be able to make a (6) balance / deposit very soon.

B Match the ways of paying with the follow-up statements. Write the letters in the box below.

1 You can pay by cash.

2 You can pay by cheque.

3 You can pay by chip and PIN.

4 You can pay by debit card.

5 You can pay by credit card.

a The money will come straight out of your account.

b You won't have to pay until next month.

c There's a cashpoint over the road if you want to get some.

d Just write your name and address on the back.

e Can you remember your number?

1	2	3	4	5

C Match six of the words from A and B with the definitions.

1 the amount of money in your bank account

2 money in the form of notes and coins

3 the paying of money into a bank account

4 machine from which you get money

5 list of money going into and out of a bank account

6 piece of paper which you sign to pay for something

17 Free time

A Match the sentence halves. Write the letters in the box below.

1	If you *are into* a hobby,	a	you meet people and enjoy yourself.
2	If you *enrol* for a class,	b	you join with other people in it.
3	If you *take part in* an activity,	c	you relax, especially after working hard.
4	If you *take up* an interest,	d	you are very interested in it.
5	If you *socialise*,	e	you start doing it regularly.
6	If you *unwind*,	f	you become a member of it.

1	2	3	4	5	6 ....

B Complete the text with the words in the box and the verbs in *italics* from A.

evening class   fan   membership   pastime   spectator sport
sports centre   stadium

When I come home from work, I like to (1) _____ with a cup of tea.
Sometimes, especially towards the end of the week, I like to go out and
(2) _____ . Otherwise, I stay at home and watch TV or read.

I didn't (3) _____ squash until five years ago, but now it's one of my
favourite hobbies. There are three courts at the local (4) _____ , and I play
there. It isn't far from my house, and (5) _____ isn't too expensive.

A lot of people who (6) _____ football both play and watch. But I'm
only interested in it as a (7) _____ – I don't (8) _____
any games myself. I've been a (9) _____ of Newcastle United since I
was a small child. I'd love to see them play in their new (10) _____ , but
I really only see them on TV.

Opera is another (11) _____ of mine. I first went to the opera about
three years ago. Once a week, I go to a two-hour (12) _____ which is
introducing me to the subject. Next year I'm going to (13) _____ on a
course about Mozart.

C Circle the correct answers.

1 People go to <u>a party / the theatre</u> to socialise.

2 People usually unwind in the <u>evening / morning</u>.

3 <u>Football / Swimming</u> is a very popular spectator sport.

4 Watching TV is probably the most popular <u>evening class / pastime</u> in the world.

5 If you take up singing, you might <u>be into / take part</u> in a concert.

6 People usually take exercise at a <u>sports centre / stadium</u>.

18 Travel

A Complete the sentences with the words in the boxes.

1 My wife's gone on a business _____ to Tokyo.

2 We went on a four-week _____ of South-east Asia.

3 My _____ to work takes half an hour.

journey
tour
trip

4 Captain Cook died on his third _____ to the Pacific.

5 We're going on a two-week Caribbean _____ .

6 The _____ from the island to the mainland takes an hour.

crossing
cruise
voyage

7 It's a 12-hour _____ from London to Bangkok.

8 My dad gave me a _____ into town.

9 If you use the motorway, it's a four-hour _____ .

drive
flight
ride

10 Sir John Hunt led the successful 1953 Everest _____ .

11 My feet hurt when I got back from the three-day _____ .

excursion
expedition
trek

12 We're going on a class _____ to York next Friday.

B Match the words from the boxes in A with the definitions.

1 journey in an aeroplane ....

2 act of travelling from one place to another ....

3 holiday on a ship in which you visit many places ....

4 journey in a car ....

5 hard journey, often on foot ....

6 journey across water ....

7 journey with a specific purpose ....

8 long journey for a special purpose ....

9 long journey by sea or in space ....

10 journey on a horse or bicycle, or in a car, bus, etc. ....

11 short journey that a group makes for pleasure ....

12 journey for pleasure in which you visit many places ....

19 Describing places

A Circle the correct words to complete the summarising sentences.

1 It's a town with houses painted pink and blue, and where there are pretty flowers everywhere. In other words, it's a <u>picturesque / unspoilt</u> town.

2 There's a market square full of people who are all very busy. In other words, there's a <u>bustling / crowded</u> market square.

3 There's a lovely beach that is quiet and private, away from people, buildings and roads. In other words, there's a lovely <u>lively / secluded</u> beach.

4 It's not a very pleasant place. It's just packed with visitors and souvenir shops. In other words, it's a very <u>quaint / touristy</u> place.

5 Our hotel was in rather bad condition. In other words, our hotel was rather <u>shabby / sleepy</u>.

6 We visited a mountain village that was a long way from anywhere else and not very easy to get to. In other words, we visited a <u>remote / seedy</u> mountain village.

B Complete the sentences with the other words from A.

1 This area is dotted with .... villages where there is little sign of life between the scorching hours of midday and four in the afternoon. At night people emerge

2 the island. This area of the city is well known for its high crime rate and many of the hotels can only be described as .... Although

3 very pretty. This is one of the world's most wonderful places, an area of the most amazing, ... natural beauty. Many people visit for the

4 and hot. Drive along the tree-lined lanes and enjoy the .... cottages you'll come across every so often. Then you

5 in the North. Along this part of the coast most of the beaches are .... We suggest you drive further south if you're looking for a quieter time. Although Many tourists prefer

6 can be busy. The harbour area has several bars, clubs and discos and is very .... at night. For a more peaceful

20 Booking a holiday

A The <u>underlined</u> words are in the wrong sentences. Write the correct word for each sentence.

1 First, think about where you want to go on holiday – your <u>high season</u>. ....

2 Read a holiday <u>itinerary</u> or two to get some ideas about places you could go. ....

3 When you book your holiday, you'll need to pay a <u>low</u> season and the full amount two weeks before you go. ....

4 You'll pay a lot more during the <u>travel insurance</u>. ....

5 Holidays are much cheaper in the <u>destination</u>. ....

6 In case you have any problems while you're away, it's wise to get <u>brochure</u>. ....

7 A week before you leave, you'll receive a detailed <u>deposit</u> with your flight times and other arrangements for your trip. ....

B Complete the sentences with the words in the box.

accommodation facilities representative resort self-catering supplement transfer

Travel agent: Sunshine Travel, can I help you?

Customer: Ah yes, I'd like to make some enquiries about a holiday to Italy, please.

Travel agent: What kind of (1) .... are you looking for?

Customer: Well, I'd prefer to cook my own meals, so I'd like a (2) .... apartment or villa, with just a basic kitchen.

Travel agent: Fine. Would you like somewhere well away from it all or do you want to be in a (3) .... with shops and restaurants, etc.

Customer: I think nearer all the (4) .... is easier when you're on holiday. Also, I wouldn't want the (5) .... from the airport to take too long.

Travel agent: You'd be just fine in one of our villas. A (6) .... from Sunshine Travel would visit you several times during your stay to make sure that everything was fine, so you'd have nothing to worry about.

Customer: Oh great. Just one other question – would I have to pay a (7) .... if I wanted to have a vegetarian meal on the flights?

Travel agent: Oh no, that would be included in the price.

Test 2 (Units 11–20)

A Complete the conversation. Write one word in each space.

A: So, has your (1) _____ of life improved since you became self-employed?

B: Oh, yes. There's much less (2) _____ , and I've managed to get a much better work-life (3) _____ .

A: How's that happened?

B: Well, I used to (4) _____ four hours a day to London, so I'm saving all that time now. I go to the sports (5) _____ every day and do yoga or an exercise class. I've also had time to take (6) _____ in things that are going on in the village.

A: Sounds as if your life is still as hectic as it was! But it must be nice being out of the (7) _____ race.

B: Yes, it is. I'm still as busy, but in a much more pleasant way. I've decided to (8) _____ on a Spanish class next term, for example. Now that I work for myself, I can have more holiday time and I want to go to South America next year. I'm going to take (9) _____ photography too. My wife's (10) _____ that, and it's something we can do together.

B Look at the jumbled letters. Find two words – a pattern and a material – and match them with the items of clothing. The letters of the words are already in order.

s p s o i t l t e k d   c h c o e t c t k e o d n
p d e l a n i n i m   f l o l i w n e r e y n
s w t o o r i p e l d   p a l t t y c e r r n e a d

1 a _____ , _____ jacket

2 _____ , _____ trousers

3 a _____ , _____ tie

4 _____ , _____ leggings

5 a _____ , _____ shirt

6 _____ , _____ jeans

28

C Replace the underlined words.

I saw an advert for a beautiful (1) set of clothes that are worn together in a magazine last week – a (2) clean, tidy and stylish silk trouser suit. I assumed it was (3) able to be washed in a washing machine, but in fact it's (4) not able to be washed in a washing machine. There's a money-back (5) promise that something will be done however, so I'm going to (6) send it back and ask for a (7) sum of money to be paid back. I'd rather have my money back than (8) change it for something similar and get another item.

1 ....
2 ....
3 ....
4 ....

5 ....
6 ....
7 ....
8 ....

D Make compound nouns with one word from each box. Then complete the sentences with the compound nouns.

account balanced bank cheque	book card diet eating
credit eating healthy junk	food habits number statement

1 I know burgers are .... – but I really love them!

2 You don't need vitamin tablets if you have a ....

3 I need a new .... I've just used my last cheque.

4 I got a leaflet about .... from the doctor's surgery.

5 If I use my .... , then I'll only pay next month.

6 Your .... is written on your debit card.

7 I changed my .... – I used to eat too late at night.

8 According to my .... , I paid the bill on the 27th.

E Circle the correct words to complete the sentences.

1 According to the itinerary / representative / transfer they sent us, we're visiting five islands.

2 It's a direct crossing / excursion / flight from London to Johannesburg.

3 The villa was quite bustling / remote / touristy – an hour's drive from the nearest town.

4 You could have a bigger room if you paid a deposit / destination / supplement.

5 In the afternoon, there's a coach drive / journey / tour of the island.

6 Horta is very lively / quaint / sleepy at night – with lots of bars and clubs.

21 Inventing things

A Put the letters in order and find six verbs connected with inventing things.

1 e v i d e s ....
2 l n a c u h ....
3 r p o d c e u ....

4 n g d e i s ....
5 v e l p o e d ....
6 d i s v o r e c ....

B Complete the text with the correct form of the verbs from A.

MONOPOLY In 1934, Charles Darrow (1) .... how to keep his friends and family entertained – he introduced them to his board game, Monopoly. The place names on the board were from Philadelphia, where he lived, and the counters were (2) .... using charms from his wife's bracelet as models. Darrow (3) .... the first 5,000 sets himself before Parker Brothers took over and (4) .... the game in 1935. It is sometiimes said that Darrow (5) .... the game from a rent-and-sale game which had been (6) .... by an Englishwoman in the 1920s.

C Complete the text with the words in the box.

forerunner   ingenious   innovations   invention   inventor
research and development   technology

VIDEO GAMES Today huge amounts of money are spent on (1) .... of the latest video games. The first one, however, was a simple game of on-screen table tennis. Its (2) .... was US physicist Willy Higinbotham, who came up with his (3) .... idea in just two weeks in 1958 for an open day at the Brookhaven National Laboratory. This was to be the (4) .... of a multi-million dollar industry.

Three years later, Steve Russell, working at Massachusetts Institute of Technology devised Spacewar, the first video computer game. This was played on a $4million computer, so was only played in universities. However, within ten years, improved (5) .... , especially the (6) .... of the microprocessor, meant that computer games could become more widespread and in 1971, the first arcade computer video game was launched by Nolan Bushnell and a company called Nutting Associates.

Atari, Bushnell's own company, created the first home video game in 1974, but since then later (7) .... , such as Nintendo Game Boy and Sony PlayStation, have taken over the market.

22 Advertising

A Complete the text with the words in the box.

advert   brand   campaign   commercial break   jingle   marketing   product
promote   publicity   slogan   target audience

Imagine that a company is preparing for the launch of a new range of pizzas. It will
often use an advertising agency for its (1) .... needs.
The advertising team have to find out if a similar (2) ....
is made by another company, what is special about this particular
(3) .... and who is likely to buy it. They then have to think of
ways to (4) .... the new pizzas – perhaps an
(5) .... on TV showing a famous chef lifting one out of the oven. The
short film may be accompanied by a (6) .... , say with Italian music, or a
(7) .... , such as 'Pizza Pizzazz, the pizza with pizzazz'. When the film is
ready, the advertising team decide the best time of day for broadcast, depending on its
(8) .... If it was aimed at children, for example, it would be shown in a
(9) .... during the day. The (10) .... may
also include further (11) .... in magazines.

B Match the words from A with the definitions.

1   giving information about something to attract
people's attention

2   a piece of information that tries to persuade
people to buy something

3   something that is made in large quantities
and sold

4   a short phrase that is easy to remember

5   advertise something to increase its sales or
popularity

6   a plan to do a number of things to achieve
a special aim

7   the name of something that is made by a
particular company

8   a short simple tune or song, used on TV

9   a short period of advertisements between
and during TV programmes

10   ways a company encourages people to buy
their things

11   people something is intended for

23 At the doctor's

A Match the **underlined** words with the definitions below.

I last went to the doctor's before I went to South-east Asia. The doctor gave me a prescription for anti-malaria tablets, but warned me that avoiding mosquito bites was the only really effective form of prevention against malaria. Apparently the infection can take up to one year to develop. If you have any illness or flu-like symptoms, such as a headache, a cough and aching muscles, especially within three months of your return home, you have to see your doctor immediately.

The doctor also told me to make an appointment with the nurse to get a vaccination against typhoid and another against Hepatitis A. I hate the thought of an injection, but I had no choice if I wanted to travel to Laos and Cambodia. I'd heard of someone who'd felt unwell and had been covered in a red rash. When his condition got worse, he'd had a blood test and this had diagnosed typhoid. Similarly, Hepatitis A is something I'd prefer to avoid. It's caused by a virus found in dirty food or water, and is infectious, so can be caught from other people with the disease.

1   the act of stopping something happening

2   area of small spots that appear on your skin when you are ill

3   piece of paper from the doctor that says what medicine you need

4   illness which has a name and is recognised by certain symptoms

5   arrangement to see someone at a particular time

6   the state someone is in

7   that can be easily passed on to another person

8   the sending out of air from your throat and mouth with a sudden, loud noise

9   the putting of a drug into someone with a needle

10   changes in your body that are signs of illness

11   a very small organism which causes disease

12   an injection to prevent someone getting a disease

13   a disease in part of your body that is caused by a bacteria or virus

14   analysis of your blood, which can identify disease

15   state of being in bad health

24 Crime

A Match the headings with the newspaper articles.

1 Arson case solved
2 Crime rate rises
3 Hunt for suspect
4 Men held after theft
5 Teenager jailed for rape
6 Police investigate assault and mugging

1	2	3
4	5	6

B Find eight types of crime in the articles and headings in A.

1 arm
2 ar
3 a
4 d
5 m
6 ra
7 s
8 t

a
Police are appealing for help in identifying a woman caught shoplifting on close circuit TV yesterday afternoon. They also want to question a witness who is known to have been entering the clothes shop in Darlington as the thief escaped.

b
Two unemployed youths have been charged with stealing a Fiat Uno after an incident outside a house in Park Drive. They will also face charges of drink driving.

c
A man was attacked as he walked home last night. The thieves ran off with his wallet. Police have released photofit pictures after the victim gave detailed descriptions of his attackers.

d
A 63-year-old widow will be sentenced next month after she admitted setting fire to her council house. This is the fourth time the woman has committed the same offence.

e
Last month there were 37 reports of crime in the Crook area compared with 26 in July, despite the introduction of a Neighbourhood Watch scheme intended to address crime prevention.

f
A 19-year-old has been imprisoned for four years for dragging a 36-year-old woman from her car at gunpoint and sexually assaulting her. The youth was also found guilty of car hijacking and armed robbery.

25 Languages

A Match the sentence halves. Write the letters in the box below.

1 If you are monolingual,

a you are able to speak a language easily, well and quickly.

2 If you are bilingual,

b you speak or use only one language.

3 If you are multilingual,

c your pronunciation is connected with your country, area or social class.

4 If you speak with an accent,

d you use words that are only spoken in your part of the country.

5 If you speak a dialect,

e you are able to use more than two languages.

6 If you are fluent,

f you are able to use two languages for communication.

| 1 | 2 | 3 | 4 | 5 | 6 |

B Complete the text with the words in the box.

body   first   foreign   international   official   second

A person's (1) _____ language (or mother tongue) is the language they learn from their parents as they are growing up. If someone moves abroad and learns the language of their new country, then this language is their (2) _____ language. Children often learn a (3) _____ language at school – British children study another European language, while children of other nationalities study English. In later life, an Italian and a Swede might use English as an (4) _____ language to communicate with each other in their work or on holiday. In some countries, where many languages are spoken, there is an (5) _____ language for formal and business use. People can also communicate without words – we can use (6) _____ language to express how we feel and what we think.

C Circle the correct answers.

1 A <u>bilingual / monolingual</u> dictionary doesn't have translations.

2 Glen (valley), and loch (lake) are examples of Scottish <u>accent / dialect</u>.

3 Hindi and English are the two <u>second / official</u> languages in India.

4 Clapping is an example of <u>body / international</u> language.

5 Bilingual secretaries usually speak their mother tongue and a <u>first / foreign</u> language.

6 Some children are <u>fluent / multilingual</u> speakers at a very early age.

26 Modern communications

A Put the words in the box into two groups.

> attachment   cc   dial   email   forward   in-box   picture messaging
> spam   subject   text message   text   voicemail

Internet

....

....

....

....

mobile phone

....

....

....

....

B Complete the text with words from A.

I begin by choosing a (1) .... for my message, for example
'Great holiday' or 'Meeting tomorrow' and then write what I want to say.
Sometimes I (2) .... the message to other people who might be
interested. Sometimes I send an (3) .... – maybe a digital photo
or something I've found on the Internet. Then, when the
(4) .... is ready to send, I (5) .... up the
Internet connection. I can look in my (6) .... to see if I've got
any new messages. I often (7) .... jokes to other people I know.
And I usually delete any (8) .... – unwanted incoming mail is
often the way you can get a virus.

C Match the text messages with their meanings. Write the letters in the box below.

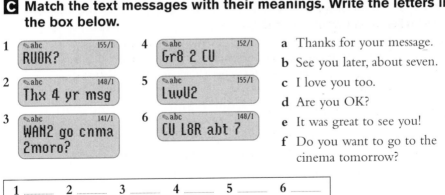

1 abc   155/1
   RUOK?

2 abc   148/1
   Thx 4 yr msg

3 abc   141/1
   **WAN2 go cnma
   2moro?**

4 abc   152/1
   Gr8 2 CU

5 abc   155/1
   LuvU2

6 abc   148/1
   CU L8R abt 7

a Thanks for your message.

b See you later, about seven.

c I love you too.

d Are you OK?

e It was great to see you!

f Do you want to go to the
   cinema tomorrow?

1 .... 2 .... 3 .... 4 .... 5 .... 6 ....

27 Using the Internet

A Circle the correct words to complete the first part of the text.

USING THE INTERNET

Looking for information on the Internet is called (1) online / surfing the Net and you need a program called a (2) browser / service provider to find and display the information. Information about each specific subject is stored in a (3) chat room / website. If you don't know the exact address you want, then a (4) modem / search engine can find useful ones for you. The first page of a site is called the (5) home page / message board and it is a directory for the web pages which follow. It also gives (6) download / links to related websites.

B Use the other words from A to complete the second part of the text.

When you find the information you're looking for, you can (1) .... it onto your computer for future reference. Sometimes you can leave a comment for other people to read on a (2) .... and exchange messages with other people in a (3) .... In order to access the Internet, you need a (4) .... which will connect your computer to the Net through a telephone line and allow you to go (5) .... You also need a (6) .... , which will provide your connection to the Internet.

C Match six of the words from A and B with the definitions.

1 a company that offers connections with the Internet ....
2 exploring the Internet ....
3 copy information into a computer's memory ....
4 a document on the Internet with pictures and text ....
5 connected to the Internet ....
6 machine used to send information from a computer through a telephone system ....

28 Personal memories

A **Complete the sentences with the words in the box.**

bring back   recall   remember   remind   reminisce   take you back

1 If you _____ something, you have something in your mind
   or you bring it back to mind.
2 If you _____ something, you try to bring a memory or
   event back to mind, especially when recounting the event to others.
3 If things _____, they make you remember a period of time.
4 If you _____ a person of someone else, you make them
   think of another person.
5 If you _____, you talk about pleasant things in the past.
6 If things _____ memories, they cause you to remember
   things.

B **The underlined words are in the wrong sentences. Write the
correct word for each sentence.**

1 In recent times, people used to walk more than
   they do now.   _____
2 Some old people can't easily recall the memorial past.   _____
3 They also become nostalgic and can't remember
   where they have put things.   _____
4 1980 was a former year for my parents – it was
   when they met.   _____
5 There was a memorable service for those killed in
   the fire.   _____
6 When I talk about my first car, I become all forgetful.   _____

C **Complete the sentences with *for*, *from*, *in*, *over* or *with* to make
expressions with the word *past*. Use one word twice.**

1 At the reunion, I recognised a couple of people _____ *the distant past.*
2 My relatives used to live in Ireland _____ *years past.*
3 I knew _____ *past experience* that he wouldn't remember my birthday.
4 Her memory has been getting worse _____ *the past two years.*
5 I don't know exactly what he did, but he's said to be a man _____ *a past.*
6 My grandmother has lived in an old people's home _____ *some time past.*

29 Notices

A Match the words from the notices with the definitions.

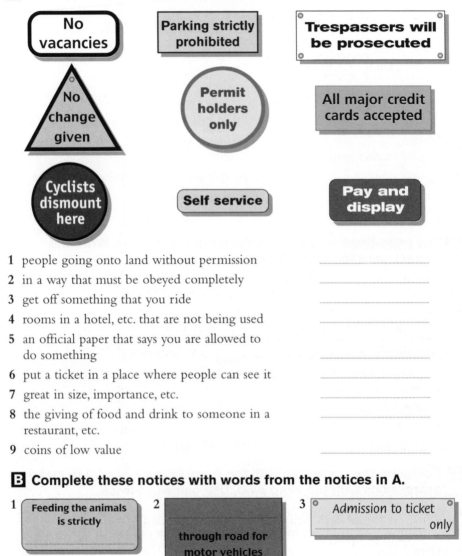

No vacancies

Parking strictly prohibited

Trespassers will be prosecuted

No change given

Permit holders only

All major credit cards accepted

Cyclists dismount here

Self service

Pay and display

1 people going onto land without permission ....

2 in a way that must be obeyed completely ....

3 get off something that you ride ....

4 rooms in a hotel, etc. that are not being used ....

5 an official paper that says you are allowed to do something ....

6 put a ticket in a place where people can see it ....

7 great in size, importance, etc. ....

8 the giving of food and drink to someone in a restaurant, etc. ....

9 coins of low value ....

B Complete these notices with words from the notices in A.

1 Feeding the animals is strictly ....

2 .... through road for motor vehicles

3 Admission to ticket .... only

4 Spanish spoken

5 Path for pedestrians and .... only

6 Shoplifters will be

30 Abbreviations

A Read the parts of the letter and complete the sentences.

1 _____ is short for 'reference'.

2 _____ is short for 'that is'.

3 _____ is short for 'please turn over'.

4 _____ is used to mean 'the letter is about this subject'.

5 _____ is used before your name if someone signs the letter for you.

6 _____ is used to mean 'copies are being sent to these people'.

Your ref:
Our ref: IL / Bk / 005

Production Manager
Strikes Management
Box 579
Liverpool WC3 5HP   June 15th 200

Dear Sir or Madam

Re: Visit to Liverpool

I am planning a visit to Liverpool next month and would be grateful

it would be possible to meet during that time, i.e. on July 3 or 4?
                                                              PTO

I look forward to hearing from you.

Yours faithfully

Jane Smith

pp *Jan Lees*

Buyer

cc Jessica Cripps, Edward Conway

B What do the abbreviations in these sentences stand for?

1 Please get in touch asap.   _____ possible

2 FYI I'm staying at the Curran Hotel.   _____ information

3 FAO Kevin Phillips, Credit Controller   _____ of

4 Please write to me c/o Dr A. J. Duncan   _____

5 cont page 20   _____

6 enc: next season's brochure   _____

A Complete the text. Write one word in each space.

There's been a lot of (1) _____ recently for 'Edison', the new film about the (2) _____ of the light bulb. I saw an (3) _____ in the paper today and there was something about it on TV the other day. Apparently the (4) _____ audience is 11 to 16-year-olds, so the film company want to (5) _____ it in schools. Another important (6) _____ of Thomas Edison's was the phonograph, the (7) _____ of the record player. I know that we've moved on since the record player and that the CD player is a more recent (8) _____ , but our modern recording industry (9) _____ from the phonograph.

B What are the crimes?

1 intentionally starting a fire in order to damage a building ....

2 attacking someone and stealing their money ....

3 taking goods from a shop without paying for them ....

4 suddenly and violently attacking someone ....

5 taking money or property illegally, often using a gun ....

6 dishonestly taking something which belongs to someone else and keeping it ....

C Circle the correct words to complete the text.

My friend Annalinda has an Italian mother and a British father and she has been (1) bilingual / monolingual / multilingual since the day she began to talk. She is equally (2) fluent / foreign / memorial in both Italian and English, and she has a bit of a Scottish (3) language / accent / dialect too because she spent part of her childhood in Edinburgh. She's great at languages. I'll always (4) remember / remind / reminisce what she did for me when we were on a (5) forgetful / former / recent holiday in Portugal. I had a chest (6) cough / disease / infection and had to stay in the tent while she went out for the day. When she came back, my (7) condition / injection / virus had got worse, so she went and found a doctor. Then she went to the chemist with the (8) vaccination / prescription / prevention he wrote out for me. I don't know what I would have done without her.

D Complete the conversation. Write one word in each space.

A: Have you checked your (1) _____ this morning?

B: Yes, I switched on my computer about ten minutes ago.

A: Did you get the one Jim sent? The (2) _____ was 'Plans for expansion'.

B: No, I don't think so. I didn't see it in my (3) _____ at any rate.

A: It was very interesting. I'll (4) _____ it to you then. He mentions a company called David Cripps & Co. You like to (5) _____ the Net, don't you?

B: Yeah, I do.

A: Well, could you go (6) _____ and find me some information about them? I'm pretty sure they'll have a (7) _____ .

B: OK, then. I'll (8) _____ whatever I find, and I'll print it out.

A: No, don't do that. Send it to me as an (9) _____ . That would be better. And could you (10) _____ it to Jim?

B: Yes, of course.

E Which of these signs might you see on a shop door? Tick the boxes.

1 No change given for parking meters ☐

2 Admission to ticket holders only ☐

3 Shoplifters will be prosecuted ☐

4 All major credit cards accepted ☐

5 German spoken here ☐

6 No vacancies ☐

7 Pay and display ☐

8 Food strictly prohibited ☐

F Write abbreviations.

1 please turn over _____

2 as soon as possible _____

3 for the attention of _____

4 for your information _____

5 that is _____

6 reference _____

7 care of _____

8 enclosed _____

31 Making countable nouns

A Complete the expressions with the words in the box.

| ball | crowd | drop | grain | item | pane | roll | sheet |

1 .... of clothing
2 .... of people
3 .... of glass
4 .... of string
5 .... of sticky tape
6 .... of paper
7 .... of blood
8 .... of sand

B Join pairs of words to make expressions for talking about the weather.

1 clap   lightning
2 flash   of   rain
3 gust   thunder
4 shower   wind

C Complete the sentences with expressions from A and B.

1 When I got to the station, there was a .... waiting on the platform.

2 Write your name at the top of the .... before you begin the exam.

3 I heard a .... overhead and then it started to rain.

4 If you want to mend that torn page, there's a .... in the top drawer.

5 It was only a light ...., so I didn't get very wet.

6 The old lady bent down to pick up the shopping list she had dropped, but a .... blew it into the road.

7 A rainproof jacket is a useful .... when you're travelling.

8 When I saw a .... on my chin, I realised I'd cut myself when I was shaving.

32 Expressions of time

A Complete the expressions of time with the words in the box.

| any at behind good in near now |
| schedule short soon term the |

1 in _____ time

2 in the _____ future

3 every _____ and again

4 _____ schedule

5 as _____ as possible

6 _____ no time

7 _____ the time

8 in the _____ term

9 in the long _____

10 _____ minute now

11 the sooner _____ better

12 on _____

B Complete the sentences with the expressions from A.

1 They are now three years _____ with the building of the motorway.

2 I don't eat much chocolate, but I like to have some _____ .

3 When I go abroad, I like to get to the airport _____ . I don't want to miss the plane.

4 I've got to get a new hair drier _____ . I can't manage without one.

5 We walked quickly and got to the station _____ .

6 The receptionist asked me when I'd like an appointment and I told her _____ .

7 We've heard that the sports centre is going to close down _____ . We're not sure where we'll go swimming.

8 I bought my bike five years ago. I didn't have a car _____ .

9 Having a filling will solve the problem _____ , but I'll need to have the tooth taken out one day.

10 The work is _____ and will be delivered tomorrow as planned.

11 My dad's just gone to the post box. He'll be back _____ .

12 The roadworks mean long queues at the moment, but travel will be easier _____ .

33 *Do and make*

A Put the words in the box into two groups.

business progress time a course a decision a difference
a good job a living a lot of damage a promise an effort
the shopping your best your homework

do   **make**

....

....

....

....

B Complete the sentences with the words from A and the correct form of *do* or *make*.

1 Work is very slow at the moment – I don't think we're
   .... at all.

2 You've .... cleaning the bathroom. Thanks very much!

3 If you .... and worked harder, you'd do much better in
   your exams.

4 I'm thinking of .... at the local college, but I'm not sure
   which subject to choose.

5 He was disappointed that she didn't help him – she had ....
   and now she was saying there was nothing she could do.

6 You can't spend any longer thinking about it. You have to ....
   – is it to be yes or no?

7 I .... once a week at the local supermarket.

8 This place looks great now. Painting the walls that colour has really
   ....

9 The fire at the restaurant has .... to the furniture and
   kitchen equipment.

10 Even if you're both very busy, it's important for your relationship that you
    .... to do things together now and again.

11 It doesn't matter that you didn't win. What's important is that you
    ....

12 Have you .... yet? We have to hand it in tomorrow.

13 You can earn a little money doing that kind of work, but you can't actually
    ....

14 My uncle's company .... with a lot of customers in Asia.

34 Phrasal verbs: studying

A Complete the phrasal verbs with *up* or *out*.

1 My brother decided to drop .... of university because he wanted to travel.

2 I missed some lessons last week, so I need to catch .... at the weekend.

3 We've got a test on Monday, so I must swot .... for it.

4 The teacher asked one of the students to hand .... a sheet of paper to each person.

5 The level is too high – I can't keep ....

6 That course looks interesting – I think I'll sign .... for it.

7 Could you find .... how many people speak English as a second language?

8 The students studied several examples and tried to work .... the difference between 'say' and 'tell'.

B Complete the phrasal verbs with *down*, *in*, *up* or *out*. Use two words twice.

1 If you copy a list of words from the board, you copy it ....

2 If you check the meaning of a word in a dictionary, you look it ....

3 If you read your essay to the class, you read it ....

4 If you raise your hand when you know the answer, you put it ....

5 If you write a new word in your vocabulary notebook, you write it ....

6 If you give your notebook to the teacher for marking, you hand it ....

C Complete the sentences with phrasal verbs from A and B.

1 You can .... the answers in the key.

2 Please don't .... your homework a day late.

3 Look at these sentences with the superlatives. Can anyone .... when we use 'most'?

4 Natalia, could you .... these grammar books for me? One between two should be OK.

5 I'll .... the phone number if you can read it out to me.

6 Can you .... for the trip to the British Museum if you want to go?

7 Listen, everyone! Amelie will .... the first part of the story.

8 If you use your dictionary, you'll .... what 'fragile' means.

35 Phrasal verbs: socialising

A Circle the correct phrasal verbs to complete the paragraph.

The other day I (1) <u>asked her out / bumped into</u> an old schoolfriend of mine, Sally Barber, while I was at the cashpoint. I hadn't seen her for ages. I wanted to (2) <u>catch up / hit it off</u> with her, so I suggested going for a cup of coffee. Unfortunately, Sally's a very busy woman, so she didn't have time for a coffee. Let's (3) <u>chat her up / meet up</u> later in the week, I suggested. Sally looked in her diary and said we could (4) <u>fit in / get together</u> for lunch at 1 pm on Friday at her favourite restaurant. It was a very smart place, so I had to (5) <u>dress up / hang out</u> for the occasion. I arrived at the restaurant in good time. I'd finished my dessert by the time she (6) <u>fell out / turned up</u> – only an hour late!

B Use the other phrasal verbs from A to complete the paragraph.

I remember how I met my wife. I used to (1) _____ with a group of friends in the summer holidays. One day, my friend Pete came along with his cousin Susie and her friend Jane, both girls about our age. Susie had nothing in common with the other people in the group, so she didn't (2) _____ at all. Jane, however, loved swimming and sport, and I (3) _____ with her at once. After a couple of days, I (4) _____ and she said yes. We went to the cinema without the others. Soon after that, I (5) _____ with Pete and we didn't speak again for a long time. I didn't know what was wrong at the time, but later Jane told me that he'd tried to (6) _____. She also told me that she wasn't interested in him, which was nice!

C Match six of the phrasal verbs from A and B with these definitions.

1 quarrel or fight (with someone)   ....

2 meet (someone) by chance   ....

3 like someone when you first meet   ....

4 invite someone to a place   ....

5 arrive   ....

6 spend a lot of time with someone   ....

36 Idioms: *hands* and *feet*

A Complete the idioms with *hand*, *hands*, *foot* or *feet*. Use each word twice.

1 Things *got out of* _____ and the teacher had to tell everyone to be quiet.

2 I didn't know that David was her brother. I really *put my* _____ *in it* when I said I didn't like him.

3 I'll *give you a* _____ with those dishes. Shall I dry?

4 At first I said I'd give a presentation. Then I *got cold* _____ and said I wasn't so sure.

5 I'd love to *get my* _____ on a ticket for Justin Timberlake. His gigs are all sold out.

6 After a hard day at work, I just wanted to *put my* _____ *up* when I got home.

7 My sister's always using my car. But this time I *put my* _____ *down* and said no.

8 My cousin has a full-time job and four children. She *has her* _____ *full*.

B Circle the correct words to complete the idioms.

1 There's something wrong with my car. I can't <u>*put / set*</u> *my finger on it.*

2 I tidied the house myself. Jane didn't <u>*lift / use*</u> *a finger.*

3 I can look at our records. I'm afraid I don't <u>*count / have*</u> *the figures at my fingertips.*

4 They'll repair the car immediately. It'll <u>*break / cost*</u> *an arm and a leg, of course.*

5 I'm not angry with you. I just like to <u>*pull / touch*</u> *your leg.*

6 I couldn't explain where the money had gone. I didn't <u>*have / want*</u> *a leg to stand on.*

C Rewrite the <u>underlined</u> part of each sentence with an idiom from this page.

1 I'll never <u>succeed in getting</u> the CD I want.

2 Can I <u>help you</u> with the washing-up?

3 I was going to jump, then I <u>became afraid to do it</u>.

4 He often <u>jokes with me</u> about what happened that day.

5 I don't like her, but I <u>can't say the exact reason why</u>.

6 Our new DVD recorder <u>was very expensive</u>.

37 Idioms: feeling happy and sad

A Circle the correct words to complete the idioms.

1 I'm _over / under_ the moon about my exam results. They're better than I expected.

2 Susie's _on a high / low_ at the moment. Everything's going well in her new job.

3 I'm _down / up_ in the dumps. I really don't like my job at the moment.

4 My brother's _on / under_ cloud nine. He's just passed his driving test.

5 My sister's _in high / low_ spirits at the moment. Her boyfriend has left her.

6 Paul looks _down / up_ in the mouth. Has something awful happened?

7 John told me he's _on top of the ground / world_. He's fallen in love.

8 I feel a bit _in / out of_ sorts. Nothing's really wrong, but things aren't quite right.

B Put the idioms from A into two groups.

idioms which mean _happy_   idioms which mean _sad_

....

....

....

....

C How would you feel in these situations? Circle the correct idiom.

1 Would you be _down in the dumps_ or _on a high_ if you failed an exam?

2 If you won a prize in a competition, would you be _in low spirits_ or _over the moon_?

3 Would you be _on top of the world_ or _out of sorts_ if the football team you support won a cup?

4 If you didn't feel very well, would you be _out of sorts_ or _on cloud nine_?

5 Would you be _down in the mouth_ or _on a high_ if you got lots of birthday cards?

6 If your best friend moved to another city, would you be _in low spirits_ or _on top of the world_?

7 Would you be _down in the mouth_ or _over the moon_ if your favourite actor died?

8 If you got a very good mark for your work, would you be _down in the dumps_ or _on cloud nine_?

38 Similes

A Circle the correct words to complete the similes.

1 If two people or things are *like two peanuts / peas in a pod*, they are almost identical.

2 If someone *drinks like a fish / fly*, they drink too much alcohol.

3 If someone is *like a bear with a big / sore head*, they are very bad-tempered.

4 If two things are *like chalk / cream and cheese*, they are completely different from each other.

5 If someone *eats like a bird / horse*, they always eat a lot of food.

6 If someone is *like a cat / fish out of water*, they are uncomfortable because of the situation they are in.

B Complete the similes with the words in the box.

bat bird cucumber daisy dodo feather

1 On my last day of work, I felt *as free as a* _____ .

2 After a bath and a good night's sleep, I felt *as fresh as a* _____ again.

3 You haven't brought much with you. This case is *as light as a* _____ .

4 My dad's computer is *as dead as a* _____ . He's had it for more than twenty years.

5 I'd be *as blind as a* _____ if I didn't have contact lenses.

6 I thought my brother would be nervous before his driving test, but, in fact, he was *as cool as a* _____ .

C Complete the sentences with similes from A and B.

1 I felt _____ . My exams were over and I could do as I wanted.

2 I'm moody, but my sister's quite cheerful. We're _____ .

3 Even though my dad _____ , he never puts on weight.

4 My mum's been on a diet. She's _____ now.

5 I'd forgotten my glasses, so I was _____ .

6 My boss is _____ this morning. I don't know why she's so grumpy.

7 I felt _____ when I first went to live abroad. Everything was so different.

8 You're looking _____ . Aren't you nervous at all?

39 Food for thought

A Match the sentence halves. Write the letters in the box below.

1 If you *keep someone sweet*,

2 If situations *turn sour*,

3 If you do something *to the bitter end*,

4 If experiences *leave a bad taste in your mouth*,

5 If you *swallow the bait*,

6 If you *have to eat your words*,

a they become unpleasant.

b you have bad memories of them.

c you are forced to admit that something you said was wrong.

d you accept something you are only offered so that you will do something.

e you do things to please them so that they help you in the future.

f you continue until it is finished, although it is hard and takes a long time.

| 1 .... | 2 .... | 3 .... | 4 .... | 5 .... | 6 .... |

B Complete each idiom and metaphor with a word in *italics* from A.

1 If you say that something someone says is .... *grapes*, you mean that they said it because they are jealous.

2 If something that someone says is *hard to* .... , it is difficult to believe.

3 If you describe something as a .... *pill*, it isn't nice but must be accepted.

4 If you *give someone a* .... *of their own medicine*, you do the same bad thing to them that they have done to you in order to show how unpleasant it is.

5 If something is *short and* .... , it is pleasantly short.

6 If you *have your cake and* .... *it*, you have or do two good things that it is usually impossible to do at the same time.

C Complete the sentences with idioms and metaphors from A and B.

1 I continued .... although I didn't like the book.

2 You want to .... You want to pass your exams, but you want to go out every evening too.

3 I'm going to give Anna .... She's usually late when we meet, so I'm going to be late this time.

4 I want to use my brother's car next week, so I'd better .... until then.

40 Collocations: *money* and *time*

A Complete the collocations with *money* or *time*.

1 We can *save* _____ *time* _____ if we take a taxi to the railway station.

2 I often *waste* quite a bit of _____ before starting my homework.

3 We didn't *lose* any _____ on the sale of the house.

4 I'll *give* you some _____ if you need it to get a car.

5 My parents *spend* a lot of _____ working in the garden at the weekend.

6 Did your brother-in-law *make* his _____ through selling used cars?

7 We want to finish the game, but we're going to *run out of* _____ .

8 We don't *have* enough _____ for the airline tickets.

B Complete the collocations with the verbs from A.

1 Our teachers _____ *give* _____ us very little *time* to do our work.

2 I'm afraid I don't _____ *time* to help you with the dishes.

3 Does your watch _____ *time* or is it always reliable?

4 I'm very busy, but I'll _____ *time* for my parents when they visit me.

5 When some people _____ *money*, they borrow from their parents.

6 You can _____ quite a lot of *money* if you buy things in the sales.

7 How much *money* did you _____ the other evening?

8 You _____ far too much *money* on cigarettes.

C Complete the sentences with collocations from A and B. Use each verb once only.

1 I'm going to _____ *spend time* _____ in Vietnam when I go to South-east Asia.

2 We've only get ten minutes to do this, so let's not _____ talking about it.

3 They _____ to lots of charities and good causes.

4 Let's _____ for a cup of coffee before we leave.

5 I try to _____ every month, even if it's only a small amount.

6 We're going to _____ if we don't hurry up and get it finished.

7 I _____ here if you need it. Look!

8 Every time they go to the races, they _____ .

Test 4 (Units 31 –40)

A Complete each sentence with two words.

1 In the storm, I actually saw a _____ of _____ hit the building.

2 I _____ quite a bit of _____ running. I train most evenings.

3 I've opened a new bank account, because I want to _____ some _____ to buy a new car.

4 I had to buy a new _____ of _____ for our kitchen window. One of our neighbour's sons kicked his football through it.

5 How much _____ will you _____ us to do this exercise?

6 Here's a _____ of _____. My dad uses it to tie up the flowers.

B Complete each sentence with the correct form of *do* or *make* and a preposition.

1 We _____ great progress yesterday, so we got there _____ good time.

2 In 2003 I lived in London. I _____ my living as an accountant _____ the time.

3 If you _____ a secretarial course, it will be of use _____ the long term.

4 We're _____ schedule right now, but just _____ your best and don't worry about how long it will take.

5 The new windows will _____ a difference _____ no time.

6 Last month's storm _____ a lot of damage to the theatre, but the repairs are _____ schedule. It should be open next week, as planned.

C Complete the idioms with the word for part of the body. Then match the idioms with their meanings. Write the letters in the box below.

1 put your _____ in it

2 not have a _____ to stand on

3 at your _____

4 down in the _____

5 not lift a _____

6 have your _____ full

a sad

b say something by accident which upsets someone

c not help someone to do something, usually because you are lazy

d be so busy that you do not have time to do anything else

e be in a situation where you can't prove something

f easy to find

1	2	3	4	5	6

D Complete the conversation with phrasal verbs. Use the correct form of the verbs in the box and prepositions.

| bump | catch | drop | fit | hang | hit | meet | sign | work | write |

A: Guess who I (1) _____ _____ the other day?

B: No idea. Go on, tell me.

A: Sheila Dawson. You know, who (2) _____ _____ of university when we were in our second year?

B: Oh, yes, I remember.

A: We've arranged to (3) _____ _____ on Friday evening, and I wondered whether you'd like to come along too. We (4) _____ _____ it's been ten years since we last saw each other, so we've got lots to (5) _____ _____ on.

B: I can't on Friday, I'm afraid. I've just (6) _____ _____ for a photography course and that starts on Friday.

A: What about another time? I (7) _____ _____ Sheila's phone number. I can give her a ring, and we can get together another time.

B: Honestly, don't worry. I never really (8) _____ it _____ with her, I have to say. I didn't particularly like her and she didn't seem to (9) _____ _____ with our group.

A: Oh, I didn't realise that was how you felt! I used to (10) _____ _____ with her quite a bit. Where were you?

B: That was before you and I became friends!

E Underline the mistake in each idiom and simile. Write the correct word.

1 My brothers are like chalk and chocolate to look at. One's tall and fair, and the other's short and dark. _____

2 Things didn't turn bitter until the police arrived. _____

3 My doctor's appointment was little and sweet. I was there only five minutes. _____

4 Where are my glasses? I'm as blind as a bird without them. _____

5 I told him a leather jacket would make him look more handsome, but he didn't taste the bait. _____

6 My brother was involved in a mugging last week, but he managed to remain as cold as cucumber through it. _____

Answer Key

1 Names

A
1 title
2 first name
3 middle name initial

4 surname
5 maiden name
6 signature

B
1 false name
2 anonymous
3 married name

4 nickname
5 pseudonym
6 autograph

2 Family

A
1 *generations*
2 family gathering
3 siblings
4 relations
5 immediate family
6 distant relatives

7 extended family
8 only child
9 close relations
10 related
11 adopted
12 runs in the family

B
1 false
2 true
3 false
4 true
5 false
6 false

3 Describing character (1)

A
1 assertiveness
2 commitment
3 conscientiousness
4 enthusiasm
5 organisation
6 ruthlessness
7 capable
8 competitive
9 decisive
10 motivated
11 reliable
12 self-assured

B
1 committed
2 competitive
3 assertive
4 self-assured
5 ruthless
6 organised
7 reliable
8 conscientious
9 enthusiastic
10 decisive
11 capable
12 motivated

4 Describing character (2)

A
1 indecisive
2 aggressive
3 introverted
4 emotional

5 secretive
6 gullible
7 open
8 trustworthy

9 placid
10 considerate
11 stubborn
12 extroverted

13 bossy
14 moody
15 materialistic

5 Describing appearance

A

big/fat	small/thin
obese	lanky
plump	petite
stocky	skinny
well-built	slim

B
1 well-built
2 obese
3 skinny
4 stocky
5 petite
6 slim
7 lanky
8 plump

C
1 build
2 figure
3 figure
4 build
5 build
6 figure
7 build
8 figure

6 How you feel

A
1 suspicious
2 furious
3 negative
4 delighted
5 positive
6 reckless

B
1 enthusiastic about
2 amazed at
3 offended by
4 grateful for
5 ashamed of
6 impressed with

C
1 amazed at
2 grateful for
3 impressed with
4 enthusiastic about
5 offended by
6 ashamed of

7 Describing things (1)

A

positive	negative
gripping	appalling
promising	criminal
sensational	inappropriate
tremendous	outrageous
	pathetic
	ridiculous
	threatening
	unacceptable

B
1 sensational
2 inappropriate
3 outrageous
4 tremendous
5 threatening
6 unacceptable
7 gripping
8 promising
9 appalling
10 pathetic
11 ridiculous
12 criminal

8 Describing things (2)

A
1 original
2 eye-catching
3 versatile
4 ideal
5 value for money
6 sophisticated

B
1 irresistible
2 high-quality
3 stylish
4 reliable
5 practical
6 handy

9 City life

A
1 *derelict*
2 suburbs
3 built-up area
4 urban
5 deprived area
6 densely populated
7 run-down
8 developments
9 up-and-coming neighbourhood
10 commercial district
11 residential areas
12 estates
13 regeneration
14 local amenities
15 suburban

B
1 true
2 false
3 true
4 false

10 Housing problems

A
1 housing shortage
2 homelessness
3 accommodation
4 council housing
5 hostels
6 squat
7 sleep rough

B
1 first-time buyer
2 mortgage
3 tenants
4 rent
5 deposit
6 home owner
7 evict

C
1 first-time buyer
2 hostels
3 home owner
4 accommodation
5 tenant
6 mortgage

Test 1 (Units 1–10)

A
1 surname
2 married
3 first
4 initial
5 title
6 related
7 distant
8 runs
9 immediate
10 only

B 1 slim
2 obese
3 lanky
4 well-built

C 1 outrageous
2 eye-catching
3 promising
4 appalling
5 versatile
6 handy

D 1 ruthless
2 secretive
3 aggressive
4 conscientious
5 emotional
6 materialistic

E 1 furious
2 impressed
3 positive
4 grateful
5 negative
6 enthusiastic

F 1 accommodation
2 tenants
3 residential
4 amenities
5 evict
6 suburbs
7 deposit
8 mortgage

11 Modern living

A
1 lifestyle
2 under pressure
3 hectic
4 stress
5 working conditions
6 work–life balance
7 commute
8 rat race
9 quality of life
10 nine-to-five
11 downshift

B 1 an office worker
2 a secondary school teacher
3 an accountant
4 a nurse
5 a marketing manager
6 a doctor

12 Describing clothes

A

materials	patterns
linen	*spotted*
wool	striped
silk	patterned
cotton	checked
denim	plain
lycra	flowery

B 1 wool
2 lycra
3 cotton
4 silk
5 linen
6 denim

C 1 checked
2 striped
3 patterned
4 plain
5 spotted
6 flowery

13 Fashion

A 1 garment
2 designer labels
3 outfit
4 casual
5 machine washable
6 smart
7 made-to-measure
8 haute couture
9 off-the-peg
10 high-street fashions
11 trend
12 dry-clean only
13 collection

B 1 false
2 true
3 false
4 false
5 true
6 false

14 Catalogue shopping

A 1 d
2 c
3 e
4 a
5 b

B 1 delivery
2 purchase
3 offer
4 guarantee
5 return
6 refund
7 exchange
8 Order
9 order form
10 payment
11 Customer Services
12 availability

15 Eating and health

A 1 balanced diet
2 nutrition
3 healthy eating
4 nutrients
5 processed foods
6 additives
7 junk food
8 convenience foods
9 fresh produce
10 organic foods
11 GM foods
12 eating habits

B 1 Fats
2 Carbohydrate
3 Protein
4 Water
5 Fibre
6 Vitamins
7 Minerals

16 Money and banking

A 1 bank account
2 account number
3 bank statement
4 balance
5 withdrawal
6 deposit

B 1 c
2 d
3 e
4 a
5 b

C 1 balance
2 cash
3 deposit
4 cashpoint
5 (bank) statement
6 cheque

17 Free time

A 1 d
2 f
3 b
4 e
5 a
6 c

B 1 unwind
2 socialise
3 take up
4 sports centre
5 membership
6 are into
7 spectator sport
8 take part in
9 fan
10 stadium
11 pastime
12 evening class
13 enrol

C 1 a party
2 evening
3 Football
4 pastime
5 take part in
6 sports centre

18 Travel

A 1 trip
2 tour
3 journey
4 voyage
5 cruise
6 crossing
7 flight
8 ride
9 drive
10 expedition
11 trek
12 excursion

B 1 flight
2 journey
3 cruise
4 drive
5 trek
6 crossing
7 trip
8 expedition
9 voyage
10 ride
11 excursion
12 tour

19 Describing places

A 1 picturesque 4 touristy
2 bustling 5 shabby
3 secluded 6 remote

B 1 sleepy 4 quaint
2 seedy 5 crowded
3 unspoilt 6 lively

20 Booking a holiday

A 1 destination
2 brochure
3 deposit
4 high season
5 low season
6 travel insurance
7 itinerary

B 1 accommodation
2 self-catering
3 resort
4 facilities
5 transfer
6 representative
7 supplement

Test 2 (Units 11–20)

A 1 quality
2 stress / pressure
3 balance
4 commute
5 centre
6 part
7 rat
8 enrol
9 up
10 into

B 1 striped, wool
2 flowery, linen
3 spotted, silk
4 patterned, lycra
5 checked, cotton
6 plain, denim

C 1 outfit
2 smart
3 machine washable
4 dry-clean only
5 guarantee
6 return (it)
7 refund
6 exchange (it)

D 1 junk food
2 balanced diet
3 cheque book
4 healthy eating
5 credit card
6 account number
7 eating habits
8 bank statement

E 1 itinerary
2 flight
3 remote
4 supplement
5 tour
6 lively

21 Inventing things

A 1 devise
2 launch
3 produce
4 design
5 develop
6 discover

B 1 discovered
2 designed
3 produced
4 launched
5 developed
6 devised

C 1 research and development
2 inventor
3 ingenious
4 forerunner
5 technology
6 invention
7 innovations

22 Advertising

A
1 marketing
2 product
3 brand
4 promote
5 advert
6 jingle
7 slogan
8 target audience
9 commercial break
10 campaign
11 publicity

B
1 publicity
2 advert
3 product
4 slogan
5 promote
6 campaign
7 brand
8 jingle
9 commercial break
10 marketing
11 target audience

23 At the doctor's

A
1 prevention
2 rash
3 prescription
4 disease
5 appointment
6 condition
7 infectious
8 cough
9 injection
10 symptoms
11 virus
12 vaccination
13 infection
14 blood test
15 illness

24 Crime

A
1 d   4 b
2 e   5 f
3 a   6 c

B
1 armed robbery
2 arson
3 assault
4 drink driving
5 mugging
6 rape
7 shoplifting
8 theft

25 Languages

A
1 b
2 f
3 e
4 c
5 d
6 a

B
1 first
2 second
3 foreign
4 international
5 official
6 body

C
1 monolingual
2 dialect
3 official
4 body
5 foreign
6 fluent

26 Modern communications

A

Internet	mobile phone
attachment	picture messaging
cc	text message
dial	text
email	voicemail
forward	
in-box	
spam	
subject	

B
1 subject
2 cc
3 attachment
4 email
5 dial
6 in-box
7 forward
8 spam

C
1 d
2 a
3 f
4 e
5 c
6 b

27 Using the Internet

A
1 surfing the Net
2 browser
3 website
4 search engine
5 home page
6 links

B
1 download
2 message board
3 chat room
4 modem
5 online
6 service provider

C
1 service provider
2 surfing the Net
3 download
4 website
5 online
6 modem

28 Personal memories

A 1 remember
2 recall
3 take you back
4 remind
5 reminisce
6 bring back memories

B 1 former
2 recent
3 forgetful
4 memorable
5 memorial
6 nostalgic

C 1 from
2 in
3 from
4 over
5 with
6 for

29 Notices

A 1 trespassers
2 strictly
3 dismount
4 vacancies
5 permit

6 display
7 major
8 service
9 change

B 1 prohibited
2 No
3 holders
4 here
5 cyclists
6 prosecuted

30 Abbreviations

A 1 ref
2 i.e.
3 PTO
4 re
5 pp
6 cc

B 1 as soon as possible
2 for your information
3 for the attention of
4 care of
5 continued
6 enclosed

Test 3 (Units 21–30)

A 1 publicity
2 inventor
3 advert
4 target
5 promote
6 invention
7 forerunner
8 innovation
9 developed

B 1 arson
2 mugging
3 shoplifting
4 assault
5 armed robbery
6 theft

C 1 bilingual
2 fluent
3 accent
4 remember
5 recent
6 infection
7 condition
8 prescription

D 1 email
2 subject
3 in-box
4 forward
5 surf
6 online
7 website
8 download
9 attachment
10 cc

E 1, 3, 4, 5 and 8

F 1 PTO
2 asap
3 FAO
4 FYI
5 i.e.
6 ref
7 c/o
8 enc

31 Making countable nouns

A 1 item
2 crowd
3 pane
4 ball
5 roll
6 sheet
7 drop
8 grain

B 1 clap of thunder
2 flash of lightning
3 gust of wind
4 shower of rain

C 1 crowd of people
2 sheet of paper
3 clap of thunder
4 roll of sticky tape
5 shower of rain
6 gust of wind
7 item of clothing
8 drop of blood

32 Expressions of time

A 1 good
2 near
3 now
4 behind
5 soon
6 in
7 at
8 short
9 term
10 any
11 the
12 schedule

B 1 behind schedule
2 every now and again
3 in good time
4 as soon as possible
5 in no time
6 the sooner the better
7 in the near future
8 at the time
9 in the short term
10 on schedule
11 any minute now
12 in the long term

33 *Do* and *make*

A **do**
business
a course
a good job
a lot of damage
the shopping
your best
your homework

make
progress
time
a decision
a difference
a living
a promise
an effort

B 1 making progress
2 done a good job
3 made an effort
4 doing a course
5 made a promise
6 make a decision
7 do the shopping
8 made a difference
9 done a lot of damage
10 make time
11 did your best
12 done your homework
13 make a living
14 does business

34 Phrasal verbs: studying

A 1 out
2 up
3 up
4 out
5 up
6 up
7 out
8 out

B 1 down
2 up
3 out
4 up
5 down
6 in

C 1 look up
2 hand in
3 work out
4 hand out
5 write down
6 sign up
7 read out
8 find out

35 Phrasal verbs: socialising

A 1 bumped into
2 catch up
3 meet up
4 get together
5 dress up
6 turned up

B 1 hang out
2 fit in
3 hit it off
4 asked her out
5 fell out
6 chat her up

C 1 fall out
2 bump into
3 hit it off
4 ask someone out
5 turn up
6 hang out

36 Idioms: *hands* and *feet*

A 1 hand
2 foot
3 hand
4 feet
5 hands
6 feet
7 foot
8 hands

B 1 put
2 lift
3 have
4 cost
5 pull
6 have

C 1 get my hands on
2 give you a hand
3 got cold feet
4 pulls my leg
5 can't put my finger on it
6 cost (us) an arm and a leg

37 Idioms: feeling happy and sad

A 1 over
2 high
3 down
4 on
5 low
6 down
7 world
8 out of

B idioms which mean *happy*
over the moon
on a high
on cloud nine
on top of the world

idioms which mean *sad*
down in the dumps
in low spirits
down in the mouth
out of sorts

C 1 down in the dumps
2 over the moon
3 on top of the world
4 out of sorts
5 on a high
6 in low spirits
7 down in the mouth
8 on cloud nine

38 Similes

A 1 peas
2 fish
3 sore
4 chalk
5 horse
6 fish

B 1 bird
2 daisy
3 feather
4 dodo
5 bat
6 cucumber

C 1 as free as a bird
2 like chalk and cheese
3 eats like a horse
4 as light as a feather
5 as blind as a bat
6 like a bear with a sore head
7 like a fish out of water
8 as cool as a cucumber

39 Food for thought

A 1 e
2 a
3 f
4 b
5 d
6 c

B 1 sour
2 swallow
3 bitter
4 taste
5 sweet
6 eat

C 1 to the bitter end
2 have your cake and eat it
3 a taste of her own medicine
4 keep him sweet
5 hard to swallow
6 sour grapes

40 Collocations: *money* and *time*

A 1 *time*
2 time
3 money
4 money
5 time
6 money
7 time
8 money

B 1 *give*
2 have
3 lose
4 make
5 run out of
6 save
7 spend
8 waste

C 1 *spend time*
2 waste time
3 give money
4 make time
5 save money
6 run out of time
7 have money
8 lose money

Test 4 (Units 31–40)

A 1 flash, lightning
2 spend, time
3 save, money
4 pane, glass
5 time, give
6 ball, string

C 1 foot, b
2 leg, e
3 fingertips, f
4 mouth, a
5 finger, c
6 hands, d

E 1 chocolate, cheese
2 bitter, sour
3 little, short
4 bird, bat
5 taste, swallow
6 cold, cool

B 1 made, in
2 made, at
3 do, in
4 behind, do
5 make, in
6 did, on

D 1 bumped into
2 dropped out
3 meet up
4 worked out
5 catch up
6 signed up
7 wrote down
8 hit (it) off
9 fit in
10 hang out

Word List

The words in this list are British English. Sometimes we give you an important American word which means the same.

1 Names

anonymous /ə'nɒnɪməs/
autograph /'ɔːtəɡrɑːf/
false name /'fɔːls ˌneɪm/
family name /'fæməli ˌneɪm/
first name /'fɜːst ˌneɪm/
initial /ɪ'nɪʃəl/
maiden name /'meɪdən ˌneɪm/
middle name /'mɪdl ˌneɪm/
nickname /'nɪkneɪm/
pseudonym /'sjuːdənɪm/
signature /'sɪɡnətʃə/
surname /'sɜːneɪm/
title /'taɪtl/

2 Family

adopted /ə'dɒptɪd/
close relations /'kləʊs rɪ'leɪʃənz/
distant relatives /'dɪstənt 'relətɪvz/
extended family /ɪk'stendɪd 'fæməli/
family gathering /'fæməli 'ɡæðərɪŋ/
generations /ˌdʒenə'reɪʃənz/
immediate family /ɪ'miːdiət 'fæməli/
only child /'əʊnli 'tʃaɪld/
related (to sb) /rɪ'leɪtɪd/
relations /rɪ'leɪʃənz/
relatives /'relətɪvz/
runs in the family /ˌrʌnz ɪn ðə 'fæməli/
siblings /'sɪblɪŋz/

3 Describing character (1)

assertive /ə'sɜːtɪv/
capable /'keɪpəbl/
committed /kə'mɪtɪd/
competitive /kəm'petɪtɪv/
conscientious /ˌkɒntʃi'entʃəs/
decisive /dɪ'saɪsɪv/
enthusiastic /ɪnˌθjuːzi'æstɪk/

motivated /ˈməʊtɪveɪtɪd/
organised /ˈɔːgənaɪzd/
reliable /rɪˈlaɪəbl/
ruthless /ˈruːθləs/
self-assured /ˌselfəˈʃʊəd/

4 Describing character (2)

aggressive /əˈgresɪv/
bossy /ˈbɒsi/
considerate /kənˈsɪdərət/
emotional /ɪˈməʊʃənəl/
extroverted /ˈekstrəvɜːtɪd/
gullible /ˈgʌlɪbl/
indecisive /ˌɪndɪˈsaɪsɪv/
introverted /ˌɪntrəʊˈvɜːtɪd/
materialistic /məˌtɪəriəˈlɪstɪk/
moody /ˈmuːdi/
open /ˈəʊpən/
placid /ˈplæsɪd/
secretive /ˈsiːkrətɪv/
stubborn /ˈstʌbən/
trustworthy /ˈtrʌstˌwɜːði/

5 Describing appearance

build /bɪld/
figure /ˈfɪgə/
lanky /ˈlæŋki/ (negative)
obese /əʊˈbiːs/ (negative)
petite /pəˈtiːt/ (only used to describe women)
plump /plʌmp/ (often used in a friendly way to avoid using fat)
skinny /ˈskɪni/ (negative)
slim /slɪm/ (positive)
stocky /ˈstɒki/
well-built /ˌwelˈbɪlt/

6 How you feel

amazed /əˈmeɪzd/
ashamed /əˈʃeɪmd/
delighted /dɪˈlaɪtɪd/
enthusiastic /ɪnˌθjuːziˈæstɪk/
furious /ˈfjʊəriəs/
grateful /ˈgreɪtfəl/

impressed /ɪmˈprest/
negative /ˈnegətɪv/
offended /əˈfendɪd/
positive /ˈpɒzətɪv/
reckless /ˈrekləs/
suspicious /səˈspɪʃəs/

7 Describing things (1)

appalling /əˈpɔːlɪŋ/
criminal /ˈkrɪmɪnəl/
gripping /ˈgrɪpɪŋ/
inappropriate /ˌɪnəˈprəupriət/
outrageous /ˌautˈreɪdʒəs/
pathetic /pəˈθetɪk/
promising /ˈprɒmɪsɪŋ/
ridiculous /rɪˈdɪkjələs/
sensational /senˈseɪʃənəl/
threatening /ˈθretənɪŋ/
tremendous /trɪˈmendəs/
unacceptable /ˌʌnəkˈseptəbl/

8 Describing things (2)

eye-catching /ˈaɪˌkætʃɪŋ/
handy /ˈhændi/
high-quality /ˈhaɪ ˈkwɒləti/
ideal /aɪˈdɪəl/
irresistible /ˌɪrɪˈzɪstəbl/
original /əˈrɪdʒənəl/
practical /ˈpræktɪkəl/
reliable /rɪˈlaɪəbl/
sophisticated /səˈfɪstɪkeɪtɪd/
stylish /ˈstaɪlɪʃ/
value for money /ˈvæljuː fə ˈmʌni/
versatile /ˈvɜːsətaɪl/

9 City life

built-up area /ˌbɪlt ʌp ˈeəriə/
commercial district /kəˈmɜːʃəl ˈdɪstrɪkt/
densely populated /ˈdentsli ˈpɒpjəleɪtɪd/
deprived area /dɪˈpraɪvd ˈeəriə/
derelict /ˈderəlɪkt/

developments /dɪˈveləpmənts/
estates /ɪˈsteɪts/
local amenities /ˈləʊkəl əˈmiːnətiz/
neighbourhood /ˈneɪbəhʊd/
regeneration /rɪˌdʒenərˈeɪʃən/
residential areas /ˌrezɪˈdentʃəl ˈeəriəz/
run-down /ˌrʌn ˈdaʊn/
suburban /səˈbɜːbən/
suburbs /ˈsʌbɜːbz/
up-and-coming /ˌʌp ən ˈkʌmɪŋ/
urban /ˈɜːbən/

10 Housing problems
accommodation /əˌkɒməˈdeɪʃən/
first-time buyer /ˈfɜːst taɪm ˈbaɪə/
council housing /ˈkaʊntsəl ˈhaʊzɪŋ/ (US = public housing)
deposit /dɪˈpɒzɪt/
evict /ɪˈvɪkt/
homelessness /ˈhəʊmləsnəs/
home owner /ˈhəʊm ˈəʊnə/
hostel /ˈhɒstəl/
housing shortage /ˈhaʊzɪŋ ˈʃɔːtɪdʒ/
mortgage /ˈmɔːgɪdʒ/
rent /rent/
squat /skwɒt/
sleep rough /ˈsliːp ˈrʌf/
tenant /ˈtenənt/

11 Modern living
commute /kəˈmjuːt/
downshift /ˈdaʊnʃɪft/
hectic /ˈhektɪk/
lifestyle /ˈlaɪfstaɪl/
nine-to-five /ˈnaɪn tə ˈfaɪv/
quality of life /ˈkwɒləti əv ˈlaɪf/
(get out of) the rat race /ðə ˈræt ˈreɪs/
stress /stres/
(be) under pressure /ˈʌndə ˈpreʃə/
working conditions /ˈwɜːkɪŋ kənˈdɪʃənz/
work-life balance /ˈwɜːk ˈlaɪf ˈbælənts/

12 Describing clothes

cotton /'kɒtən/
denim /'denɪm/
linen /'lɪnɪn/
lycra /'laɪkrə/
silk /sɪlk/
wool /wʊl/
checked /tʃekt/
flowery /'flaʊəri/
patterned /'pætənd/
plain /pleɪn/
spotted /'spɒtɪd/
striped /straɪpt/

13 Fashion

casual /'kæʒjuəl/
collection /kə'lekʃən/
designer label /dɪ'zaɪnə 'leɪbəl/
dry-clean only /'draɪ 'kliːn 'əʊnli/
garment /'gɑːmənt/
haute couture /ˌəʊt kʊ'tjʊər/
high-street fashions /'haɪ 'striːt 'fæʃənz/
machine washable /mə'ʃiːn 'wɒʃəbl/
made-to-measure /ˌmeɪd tə 'meʒə/
off-the-peg /ˌɒf ðə 'peg/
outfit /'aʊtfɪt/
smart /smɑːt/
trend /trend/

14 Catalogue shopping

availability /əˌveɪlə'bɪləti/
Customer Services /'kʌstəmə 's3ːvɪsɪz/
delivery /dɪ'lɪvəri/
exchange /ɪks'tʃeɪndʒ/
guarantee /ˌgærən'tiː/
offer /'ɒfə/
order /'ɔːdə/
order form /'ɔːdə 'fɔːm/

payment /'peɪmənt/
purchase /'pɜːtʃəs/
refund /'riːfʌnd/
return /rɪ'tɜːn/

15 Eating and health
additives /'ædətɪvz/
balanced diet /'bælənst daɪət/
convenience foods /kən'viːniənts 'fuːdz/
eating habits /'iːtɪŋ 'hæbɪts/
fresh produce /'freʃ 'prɒdjuːs/
GM foods /'dʒiː 'em, fuːdz/
healthy eating /'helθi 'iːtɪŋ/
junk food /'dʒʌŋk ,fuːd/
nutrients /'njuːtriənts/
nutrition /njuː'trɪʃən/
organic /ɔː'gænɪk/
processed foods /'prəʊsest ,fuːdz/
carbohydrate /,kɑːbəʊ'haɪdreɪt/
fat /fæt/
fibre /'faɪbə/
minerals /'mɪnərəlz/
protein /'prəʊtiːn/
vitamins /'vɪtəmɪnz/
water /'wɔːtə/

16 Money and banking
account number /ə'kaʊnt 'nʌmbə/
balance /'bæləns/
bank account /'bæŋk ə'kaʊnt/
bank statement /'bæŋk 'steɪtmənt/
cash /kæʃ/
cashpoint /'kæʃpɔɪnt/
cheque /tʃek/
cheque book /'tʃek 'bʊk/
chip and PIN /'tʃɪp ən 'pɪn/
credit card /'kredɪt ,kɑːd/
debit card /'debɪt ,kɑːd/
deposit /dɪ'pɒzɪt/
withdrawal /wɪð'drɔːəl/

17 Free time

be into something /biː 'ɪntə 'sʌmpθɪŋ/
enrol /ɪn'rəʊl/
evening class /'iːvənɪŋ 'klɑːs/
fan /fæn/
membership /'membəʃɪp/
pastime /'pɑːstaɪm/
spectator sport /spek'teɪtə 'spɔːt/
sports centre /'spɔːts 'sentə/
stadium /'steɪdiəm/
take part in something /ˌteɪk 'pɑːt ɪn 'sʌmpθɪŋ/
take up /ˌteɪk 'ʌp/ (*past tense* took, *past participle* taken)
unwind /ʌn'waɪnd/ (*past tense* & *past participle* unwound)
socialise /'səʊʃəlaɪz/

18 Travel

crossing /'krɒsɪŋ/
cruise /kruːz/
drive /draɪv/ (*past tense* drove, *past participle* driven)
excursion /ɪk'skɜːʃən/
expedition /ˌekspɪ'dɪʃən/
flight /flaɪt/
journey /'dʒɜːni/
ride /raɪd/ (*past tense* rode, *past participle* ridden)
trek /trek/
trip /trɪp/
tour /tʊər/
voyage /'vɔɪɪdʒ/

19 Describing places

bustling /'bʌslɪŋ/
crowded /'kraʊdɪd/
lively /'laɪvli/
picturesque /ˌpɪktʃər'esk/
quaint /kweɪnt/
remote /rɪ'məʊt/
secluded /sɪ'kluːdɪd/
seedy /'siːdi/

shabby /'ʃæbi/
sleepy /'sliːpi/
touristy /'tʊərɪsti/
unspoilt /ʌn'spɔɪlt/ (US = unspoiled)

20 Booking a holiday

accommodation /əˌkɒmə'deɪʃən/
brochure /'brəʊʃə/
deposit /dɪ'pɒzɪt/
destination /ˌdestɪ'neɪʃən/
facilities /fə'sɪlətiz/
itinerary /aɪ'tɪnərəri/
high season /'haɪ 'siːzən/
low season /'ləʊ 'siːzən/
representative /ˌreprɪ'zentətɪv/
resort /rɪ'zɔːt/
self-catering /ˌself 'keɪtərɪŋ/
supplement /'sʌplɪmənt/
transfer /'trænsfɜː/
travel insurance /'trævəl ɪn'ʃʊərəns/

21 Inventing things

design /dɪ'zaɪn/
develop /dɪ'veləp/
devise /dɪ'vaɪz/
discover /dɪ'skʌvə/
forerunner /'fɔːˌrʌnə/
ingenious /ɪn'dʒiːniəs/
innovation /ˌɪnəʊ'veɪʃən/
invention /ɪn'ventʃən/
inventor /ɪn'ventə/
launch /lɔːntʃ/
produce /'prɒdjuːs/
research and development /rɪ'sɜːtʃ ən dɪ'veləpmənt/
technology /tek'nɒlədʒi/

22 Advertising

advert /'ædvɜːt/ (informal = ad)
brand /brænd/
campaign /kæm'peɪn/
commercial break /kə'mɜːʃəl 'breɪk/
jingle /'dʒɪŋgl/

marketing /'mɑːkɪtɪŋ/
product /'prɒdʌkt/
promote /prə'məʊt/
publicity /pʌb'lɪsəti/
slogan /'sləʊgən/
target audience /'tɑːgɪt 'ɔːdiəns/

23 At the doctor's
appointment /ə'pɔɪntmənt/
blood test /'blʌd 'test/
condition /kən'dɪʃən/
cough /kɒf/
disease /dɪ'ziːz/
illness /'ɪlnəs/
infection /ɪn'fekʃən/
infectious /ɪn'fekʃəs/
injections /ɪn'dʒekʃənz/
prescription /prɪ'skrɪpʃən/
prevention /prɪ'venʃən/
rash /ræʃ/
symptoms /'sɪmptəmz/
vaccination /ˌvæksɪ'neɪʃən/
virus /'vaɪrəs/

24 Crime
armed robbery /'ɑːmd 'rɒbəri/
arson /'ɑːsən/
assault /ə'sɔːlt/
charge /tʃɑːdʒ/
crime prevention /'kraɪm prɪ'venʃən/
crime rate /'kraɪm 'reɪt/
drink driving /'drɪŋk 'draɪvɪŋ/
investigate /ɪn'vestɪgeɪt/
mugging /'mʌgɪŋ/
offence /ə'fens/
photofit /'fəʊtəʊfɪt/
question /'kwestʃən/
rape /reɪp/

shoplifting /'ʃɒplɪftɪŋ/
suspect /'sʌspekt/
theft /θeft/
victim /'vɪktɪm/

25 Languages
accent /'æksənt/
bilingual /baɪ'lɪŋgwəl/
body language /'bɒdi 'læŋgwɪdʒ/
dialect /'daɪəlekt/
first language /'fɜːst 'læŋgwɪdʒ/
fluent /'fluːənt/
foreign language /'fɒrɪn 'læŋgwɪdʒ/
international language /ˌɪntə'næʃənəl 'læŋgwɪdʒ/
monolingual /ˌmɒnəʊ'lɪŋgwəl/
mother tongue /'mʌðə 'tʌŋ/
multilingual /ˌmʌlti'lɪŋgwəl/
official language /ə'fɪʃəl 'læŋgwɪdʒ/
second language /'sekənd 'læŋgwɪdʒ/

26 Modern communications
attachment /ə'tætʃmənt/
cc (carbon copy) /ˌsiː 'siː/
dial /daɪəl/
email /'iːmeɪl/
forward /'fɔːwəd/
in-box /'ɪn 'bɒks/
picture messaging /'pɪktʃə 'mesɪdʒɪŋ/
spam /spæm/
subject /'sʌbdʒɪkt/
text /tekst/
text message /'tekst 'mesɪdʒ/
voicemail /'vɔɪsmeɪl/

27 Using the Internet
browser /'braʊzə/
chat room /'tʃæt 'ruːm/
download /ˌdaʊn'ləʊd/
home page /'həʊm 'peɪdʒ/
links /lɪŋks/
message board /'mesɪdʒ ˌbɔːd/
modem /'məʊdem/

online /ˌɒnˈlaɪn/
search engine /ˈsɜːtʃ ˈendʒɪn/
service provider /ˈsɜːvɪs prəʊˈvaɪdə/
surfing the Net /ˈsɜːfɪŋ ðə ˈnet/
website /ˈwebsaɪt/

28 Personal memories

(bring back) memories /ˈmeməriz/
forgetful /fəˈgetfəl/
former /ˈfɔːmə/
memorable /ˈmemərəbl/
memorial /məˈmɔːriəl/
nostalgic /nɒsˈtældʒɪk/
recall /rɪˈkɔːl/
recent /ˈriːsənt/
remember /rɪˈmembə/
remind /rɪˈmaɪnd/
reminisce /ˌremɪˈnɪs/
take (sb) back /ˌteɪk ˈbæk/
for some time past /fə ˈsʌm ˈtaɪm ˈpɑːst/
from the distant past /ˌfrɒm ðə ˈdɪstənt ˈpɑːst/
from past experience /ˌfrɒm ˈpɑːst ɪkˈspɪəriəns/
in (years) past /ɪn pɑːst/
over the past (two years) /ˈəʊvə ðə ˈpɑːst/
with a past /ˌwɪð ə ˈpɑːst/

29 Notices

Admission to ticket holders only /ədˈmɪʃən tə ˈtɪkɪt ˈhəʊldəz ˈəʊnli/
All major credit cards accepted /ˈɔːl ˈmeɪdʒə ˈkredɪt ˈkɑːdz əkˈseptɪd/
Cyclists dismount here /ˈsaɪklɪsts dɪˈsmaʊnt ˈhɪə/
Feeding the animals strictly prohibited /ˈfiːdɪŋ ðə ˈænɪməlz ˈstrɪktli prəʊˈhɪbɪtɪd/
No vacancies /nəʊ ˈveɪkənsiz/
No change given /nəʊ ˈtʃeɪndʒ ˈgɪvən/
No through road for motor vehicles /nəʊ ˈθruː ˈrəʊd fə ˈməʊtə ˈvɪəklz/
Nothing to declare /ˈnʌθɪŋ tə dɪˈkleə/
Parking strictly prohibited /ˈpɑːkɪŋ ˈstrɪktli prəʊˈhɪbɪtɪd/
Path for pedestrians and cyclists only /pɑːθ fə pɪˈdestriənz ən ˈsaɪklɪsts ˈəʊnli/

Pay and display /'peɪ ən dɪ'spleɪ/
Permit holders only /'pɜːmɪt 'həʊldəz 'əʊnli/
Self service /'self 'sɜːvɪs/
Shoplifters will be prosecuted. /'ʃɒpˌlɪftəz wɪl biː 'prɒsɪkjuːtɪd/
Spanish spoken here /'spænɪʃ 'spəʊkən hɪər/
Trespassers will be prosecuted /'trespəsəz wɪl biː 'prɒsɪkjuːtɪd/

30 Abbreviations
asap (as soon as possible) /ˌeɪ es eɪ 'piː/
fao (for the attention of)
fyi (for your information)
cc (carbon copy) /ˌsiː 'siː/
c/o (care of) /ˌsiː 'əʊ/
cont (continued)
enc (enclosed)
i.e. (that is) /aɪ 'iː/
pp (on behalf of) /'pi 'pi/
PTO (please turn over) /ˌpiː tiː 'əʊ/
re (about) /reɪ/
ref (reference)

31 Making countable nouns
ball of string /'bɔːl əv 'strɪŋ/
clap of thunder /'klæp əv 'θʌndə/
crowd of people /'kraʊd əv 'piːpl/
drop of blood /'drɒp əv 'blʌd/
flash of lightning /'flæʃ əv 'laɪtnɪŋ/
grain of sand /'greɪn əv 'sænd/
gust of wind /'gʌst əv 'wɪnd/
item of clothing /'aɪtəm əv 'kləʊðɪŋ/
pane of glass /'peɪn əv 'glɑːs/
roll of sticky tape /'rəʊl əv 'stɪki 'teɪp/
sheet of paper /'ʃiːt əv 'peɪpə/
shower of rain /'ʃaʊər əv 'reɪn/

32 Expressions of time
any minute now /'eni mɪ'nɪt naʊ/
as soon as possible /æz 'suːn æz 'pɒsəbl/
at the time /æt ðə 'taɪm/
behind schedule /bɪ'haɪnd 'ʃedjuːl/
every now and again /'evri naʊ ənd ə'gen/
in good time /ɪn 'gʊd 'taɪm/

in no time /ɪn ˈnəʊ ˌtaɪm/
in the long term /ɪn ðə ˈlɒŋ ˈtɜːm/
in the near future /ɪn ðə ˈnɪə ˈfjuːtʃə/
in the short term /ɪn ðə ˈʃɔːt ˌtɜːm/
on schedule /ɒn ˈʃedjuːl/
the sooner the better /ðə ˈsuːnə ðə ˈbetə/

33 *Do* and *make*

do your best /ˌduː ˈjɔː ˈbest/ (*past tense* did, *past participle* done)
do business /ˌduː ˈbɪznɪs/
do a course /ˌduː ə ˈkɔːs/
do a lot of damage /ˌduː ə ˈlɒt əv ˈdæmɪdʒ/
do a good job /ˌduː ə ˈgʊd ˈdʒɒb/
do your homework /ˌduː jɔː ˈhəʊmwɜːk/
do the shopping /ˌduː ðə ˈʃɒpɪŋ/
make a decision /ˌmeɪk ə dɪˈsɪʒən/ (*past tense* & *past participle* made)
make a difference /ˌmeɪk ə ˈdɪfərəns/
make an effort /ˌmeɪk ən ˈefət/
make a living /ˌmeɪk ə ˈlɪvɪŋ/
make progress /ˌmeɪk ˈprəʊgres/
make a promise /ˌmeɪk ə ˈprɒmɪs/
make time /ˌmeɪk ˈtaɪm/

34 Phrasal verbs: studying

catch up /ˌkætʃ ˈʌp/ (*past tense* & *past participle* caught)
copy (sth) down /ˌkɒpi ˈdaʊn/
drop out /ˌdrɒp ˈaʊt/
find out /ˌfaɪnd ˈaʊt/ (*past tense* & *past participle* found)
hand in /ˌhænd ˈɪn/
hand out /ˌhænd ˈaʊt/
keep up /ˌkiːp ˈʌp/ (*past tense* & *past participle* kept)
look (sth) up /ˌlʊk ˈʌp/
put up /ˌpʊt ˈʌp/ (*past tense* & *past participle* put)
read (sth) out /ˌriːd ˈaʊt/ (*past tense* & *past participle* read)
sign up /ˌsaɪn ˈʌp/
swot up /ˌswɒt ˈʌp/
work out /ˌwɜːk ˈaʊt/
write (sth) down /ˌraɪt ˈdaʊn/ (past tense *wrote*, past participle *written*)

35 Phrasal verbs: socialising

ask (sb) out /ˌɑːsk ˈaʊt/
bump into /ˌbʌmp ˈɪntə/

catch up /ˌkætʃ ˈʌp/ (*past tense & past participle* caught)
chat (sb) up /ˌtʃæt ˈʌp/
dress up /ˌdres ˈʌp/
fall out /ˌfɔːl ˈaʊt/ (*past tense* fell, *past participle* fallen)
fit in /ˌfɪt ˈɪn/ (*past tense & past participle* fit)
get together /ˌget təˈgeðə/ (*past tense & past participle* got)
hang out /ˌhæŋ ˈaʊt/ (*past tense & past participle* hung)
hit it off /ˌhɪt ˌɪt ˈɒf/ (*past tense & past participle* hit)
meet up /ˌmiːt ˈʌp/ (*past tense & past participle* met)
turn up /ˌtɜːn ˈʌp/

36 Idioms: *hands* and *feet*

at your fingertips /ˌæt jɔː ˈfɪŋgətɪps/
cost an arm and a leg /ˈkɒst ən ˈɑːm ənd ə ˈleg/
get cold feet /ˌget ˈkəʊld ˈfiːt/
get out of hand /ˌget aʊt əv ˈhænd/
get your hands on (sth) /ˌget jɔː ˈhændz ɒn /
give (sb) a hand /ˌgɪv ə ˈhænd/
have your hands full /ˌhæv jɔː ˈhændz ˈfʊl/
not have a leg to stand on /nɒt ˌhæv ə ˈleg tə ˈstænd ɒn/
not lift a finger /nɒt ˌlɪft ə ˈfɪŋgə/
pull sb's leg /ˌpʊl ˈsʌmwʌnz leg/
put your foot down /ˌpʊt jɔː ˈfʊt ˈdaʊn/
put your foot in it /ˌpʊt jɔː ˈfʊt ɪn ɪt/
put your feet up /ˌpʊt jɔː ˈfiːt ʌp/
put your finger on (sth) /ˌpʊt jɔː ˈfɪŋgər ɒn/

37 Idioms: feeling happy and sad

on cloud nine /ɒn ˈklaʊd ˈnaɪn/
on a high /ɒn ə ˈhaɪ/
on top of the world /ɒn ˈtɒp əv ðə ˈwɜːld/
over the moon /ˈəʊvə ðə ˈmuːn/
down in the dumps /ˈdaʊn ɪn ðə ˈdʌmps/
down in the mouth /ˈdaʊn ɪn ðə ˈmaʊθ/
in low spirits /ɪn ˈləʊ ˈspɪrɪts/
out of sorts /ˌaʊt əv ˈsɔːts/

38 Similes

as blind as a bat /æz ˈblaɪnd æz ə ˈbæt/
as cool as a cucumber /æz ˈkuːl æz ə ˈkjuːkʌmbə/
as dead as a dodo /æz ˈded æz ə ˈdəʊdəʊ/
as free as a bird /æz ˈfriː æz ə ˈbɜːd/

as fresh as a daisy /æz 'freʃ æz ə 'deɪzi/
as light as a feather /æz 'laɪt æz ə 'feðə/
drink like a fish /ˌdrɪŋk ˌlaɪk ə 'fɪʃ/
eat like a horse /ˌiːt ˌlaɪk ə 'hɔːs/
like a bear with a sore head /ˌlaɪk ə 'beə wɪð ə 'sɔː 'hed/
like a fish out of water /ˌlaɪk ə 'fɪʃ aʊt əv 'wɔːtə/
like chalk and cheese /ˌlaɪk 'tʃɔːk ən 'tʃiːz/
like two peas in a pod /ˌlaɪk tuː 'piːz ɪn ə 'pɒd/

39 Food for thought

a bitter pill /ə 'bɪtə 'pɪl/
eat your words /'iːt jɔː 'wɜːdz/
give someone a taste of their own medicine /ˌgɪv 'sʌmwʌn ə 'teɪst əv ðeər
əʊn 'medsən/
hard to swallow /ˌhɑːd tə 'swɒləʊ/
have your cake and eat it /ˌhæv jɔː 'keɪk ənd 'iːt ɪt/
keep someone sweet /ˌkiːp 'sʌmwʌn 'swiːt/
leave a bad taste in your mouth /ˌliːv ə ˌbæd 'teɪst ɪn jɔː 'maʊθ/
short and sweet /'ʃɔːt ən 'swiːt/
sour grapes /'saʊə 'greɪps/
swallow the bait /'swɒləʊ ðə 'beɪt/
to the bitter end /tə ðə 'bɪtər 'end/
turn sour /ˌtɜːn 'saʊə/

40 Collocations: *money* and *time*

give (sb) money /ˌgɪv 'mʌni/
have money /ˌhæv 'mʌni/
lose money /ˌluːz 'mʌni/
make money /ˌmeɪk 'mʌni/
run out of money /ˌrʌn aʊt əv 'mʌni/
save money /ˌseɪv 'mʌni/
spend money /ˌspend 'mʌni/
waste money /ˌweɪst 'mʌni/
give (sb) time /ˌgɪv 'taɪm/
have time /ˌhæv 'taɪm/
lose time /ˌluːz 'taɪm/
make time /ˌmeɪk 'taɪm/
run out of time /ˌrʌn aʊt əv 'taɪm/
save time /ˌseɪv 'taɪm/
spend time /ˌspend 'taɪm/
waste time /ˌweɪst 'taɪm/

Acknowledgements

We are very grateful to all the schools, institutions, teachers and students around the world who either piloted or commented on the material:

Guitar Chou, Taiwan
Ludmila Gorodetskaya, Russia
Magdalena Kijak, Poland
Andrew Maggs, Japan

The authors would like to thank Martine Walsh at Cambridge University Press for her help, guidance and support during the writing of this series. Their thanks also to Ruth Carim for her excellent proofreading, and to Kamae Design and Kate Charlesworth for their excellent design and artwork.

The publisher would like to thank the following for permission to reproduce photographs:
p.6 Alamy Images (Ace Stock Limited); p.15 (Adam Shimali/Image State); p.21 (Elizabeth Whiting & Associates); p.27 Stone/Getty Images (Bob Thomas); p.46 Powerstock (Javier Larrea/age fotostock).

Vocabulary in Practice

	SBN-10	SBN-13
Level 1 Beginner	0521 010802	978 0521 010801
Level 2 Elementary	0521 010829	978 0521 010825
Level 3 Pre-intermediate	0521 753759	978 0521 753753
Level 4 Intermediate	0521 753767	978 0521 753760
Level 5 Intermediate to upper-intermediate	0521 601258	978 0521 601252
Level 6 Upper-intermediate	0521 601266	978 0521 601269

Grammar in Practice

	SBN-10	SBN-13
Level 1 Beginner	0521 665760	978 0521 665766
Level 2 Elementary	0521 665663	978 0521 665667
Level 3 Pre-intermediate	0521 540410	978 0521 540414
Level 4 Intermediate	0521 540429	978 0521 540421